Social Action and Power

Social Action and Power

FRANCO CRESPI

BLACKWELL
Oxford UK & Cambridge USA

Copyright © Società editrice Il Mulino, Bologna, 1989

First published in 1989 as *Azione Sociale e Potere* by Società editrice Il Mulino SpA,
Bologna, Italy

The right of Franco Crespi to be identified as author of this work has been
asserted in accordance with the Copyright, Designs and Patents Act 1988.

First published in English in 1992

Blackwell Publishers
108 Cowley Road
Oxford OX4 1JF
UK

238 Main Street, Suite 501
Cambridge, Massachusetts 02142
USA

All rights reserved. Except for the quotation of short passages for the
purposes of criticism and review, no part of this publication may be
reproduced, stored in a retrieval system, or transmitted, in any form or by
any means, electronic, mechanical, photocopying, recording or otherwise,
without the prior permission of the publisher.

Except in the United States of America, this book is sold subject to the
condition that it shall not, by way of trade or otherwise, be lent, resold,
hired out, or otherwise circulated without the publisher's prior consent in
any form of binding or cover other than that in which it is published and
without a similar condition including this condition being imposed on the
subsequent purchaser.

British Library Cataloguing in Publication Data

A CIP catalogue record for this book is available from the British Library.

Library of Congress Cataloging-in-Publication Data

Crespi, Franco.
    [Azione sociale e potere. English]
    Social action and power/Franco Crespi.
    p. cm.
    Translation of: Azione sociale e potere.
    Includes bibliographical references and index.
        ISBN 0-631-18232-2 (hb: alk. paper).—
  ISBN 0-631-18233-0 (pbk.; alk. paper)
    1. Social interaction. 2. Power (Social sciences) I. Title.
HM291.C6913 1992
302—dc20

                                                          92-6017
                                                            CIP

Typeset in 11 on 13 pt Garamond by Best-set Typesetter Ltd., Hong Kong
Printed in Great Britain by T.J. Press (Padstow) Ltd., Padstow, Cornwall

This book is printed on acid-free paper

Contents

Foreword by Zygmunt Bauman — vii

Author's Note — xi

Introduction — 1

1 In Search of Action — 5
  1.1 Action and behaviour — 5
  1.2 Action and social system — 9
  1.3 Rationality and the theory of action — 14
  1.4 Action and labour — 25
  1.5 Action and the subject–structure relation — 30
  1.6 Action and communication — 35
  1.7 Where to find action — 47

2 Action as a Borderline Concept — 52
  2.1 The reduction of action to meaning — 52
  2.2 Observance of rules and relation to rules — 54
  2.3 The revival of the philosophy of praxis — 60
  2.4 Life-world and anonymous intentionality — 62
  2.5 The ontology of understanding and the hermeneutic circle — 64
  2.6 Existential phenomenology and hermeneutics — 71
  2.7 Hermeneutics and pragmatism — 75

3	General Categories of Action	81
	3.1 Action and desire	81
	3.2 Insecurity and identity	86
	3.3 Action as involvement: care and responsibility	90
	3.4 Action and transcendence	92
4	Power	95
	4.1 Sociality and normative order	96
	4.2 Inner power	100
	4.3 Outer power	104
	4.4 Structural power and the production of inequality	111
	4.5 Structural power and social system: the crises of power	114
	4.6 Theories of power and theory of action	116
5	Problems of Method	119
	5.1 Hermeneutics and scientific discourse	119
	5.2 The phenomenological analysis of action	124
	5.3 Social research in a hermeneutic perspective	127
6	Some Conclusions	133
References		138
Index		145

Foreword

Franco Crespi's timely study aims at the very heart of contemporary sociological discourse. Indeed, no other controversy in the long history of social science has proved to be so persistent, so resilient to endlessly proposed solutions, so dismissive of compromise suggestions, and so rich in methodological and theoretical consequences. No other debate has engaged as many (virtually all) leading minds of the discipline. None has been found so central to the strategy of social study in all its fields and forms.

Since Talcott Parsons's epoch-making *Structure of Social Action*, the mystery of social action at once *voluntary* and *patterned* has remained the most haunting of the unresolved theoretical problems of sociology. If human action is free, purposeful and motivated, how is it that a relatively stable and essentially predictable pattern of conduct persists over long stretches of time? If societies display 'structures' – durable patterns of human relations – how can this fact be squared with the common intuition of a voluntary character of all, or almost all, human behaviour? And can one have a theory which gives full justice, simultaneously, to both, clearly incompatible, features of social reality?

Of course, these questions were not new even at the time Parsons wrote the book which firmly established him as the leading theorist of the post-war decades; only the formulation was original. The question itself went back to the beginnings of modern sociology, when a choice seemed to be necessary between the 'individual' and the 'society' as the decisive unit of social analysis. Is all social 'totality' but a by-product, solid or illusory, of many individuals each in hot pursuit of his/her personal ends, be it happiness, gain, power, prestige or whatever else may bring pleasure? Or is it, on the contrary, the social group that by hook or by crook, through coercion, indoctrination or silent and invisible conditioning, shapes and guides and prompts every step the individual takes allegedly on his/her own initiative and free choice? For some sociologists, only the individual actor was 'real', and so in order to explain any form or event of social life one had to refer it ultimately to the motives residing in individual minds. For others, all roots of human reality were firmly set in society, which was for that reason the only valid object of study and analysis. Social behaviour could only be explained by social, supra-individual forces: tell me where and how a given individual, or a given category of individuals, is located in society, and I'll tell you what he/they are likely to do. Still other sociologists wished earnestly to square the circle: both individuals and society are important as both have qualities of their own, not fully reducible to each other, and none is fully determined by or independent of the other. That middle-of-the-road proposition seemed intuitively the least vulnerable theoretically and thus the most promising methodologically. Unfortunately, its proponents rarely ventured beyond stating their conviction in the most general of ways. Their declarations of intent, however attractively and cogently phrased, were of little help to practising sociologists eager to follow the advice in their research.

The importance of Parsons's reformulation of the old problem of 'individual vs. society' consisted in bringing the debate closer to the research problems confronted by the social scientist: in its new form the old dilemma seemed to be easier to translate into a research programme, and even, perhaps, to generate ultimately a contradiction-free theoretical model. That much Parsons himself promised in his study of social action.

Parsons's innovation expressed itself in starting from the very point which other theorists struggled laboriously to reach at the end of their investigations; namely, by accepting as a 'brute fact' that action is both voluntary and patterned, and only then asking the question: 'What conditions must necessarily be met for that apparently incongruous, yet evidently true fact to be possible?' For many reasons, acutely analysed by Crespi, this well-intentioned programme failed to deliver on its promise. If anything, Parsons's effort demonstrated the inherent danger of veering towards one or other of the poles of the old dilemma which – apparently rooted in the starting point – reveals itself the moment one attempts to spell out the sought-after conditions under which the analytical polarity of action could be proved false, or at least rendered methodologically harmless.

Parsons failed to resolve the issue to everybody's satisfaction. The long debate did not grind to a halt. On the contrary, in recent years it has gained considerably in vigour, being universally recognized as a pivotal issue in the ongoing reorientation of sociological theory and the strategy of social science. Most recently, the debate has become increasingly sophisticated and philosophically refined, thanks principally to the theory of 'structuration' developed by the outstanding British theorist Anthony Giddens. As one would expect, the more densely populated the field, the more difficult it becomes, not just for a newcomer but also for a seasoned traveller, to take cognizance of the territory and to find a way through to the intended destination.

It is for everybody, therefore – for professional sociologists and novices of the discipline alike – that Franco Crespi offers invaluable assistance. He provides a superb chart of a crucial and vast area of controversy, a chart better than most others recently written or likely soon to be written, as he steps decisively beyond the confines of any one national tradition or linguistic circle, bringing into the picture everything of importance that has been considered in all the major centres of contemporary social study. Crespi's astounding erudition is second to none, as he moves with equal ease through Anglo-Saxon, French, German and Italian approaches to the issue, many of which are little known or remain thus far unjustly neglected outside their own country. Few sociologists would be capable of drawing on so many sources while assigning to each its properly calculated weight, a function of its substantive importance rather than its linguistic accessibility.

However gratifying Crespi's study may be when read as an historical survey and a 'career report' of the social action debate, it has yet more to offer its readers. Crespi's goal is synthesis: he aims to bring together the disparate treatments of the issue that abound in contemporary literature, reducing their overt disagreements to a level at which they can communicate with each other and reach consensus. Of course, this is not the first attempt of its kind. Many have been undertaken before; still more will be tried in the future. One cannot predict that Crespi's proposal will be final, though this is what each successive exercise in synthesis aims to be. The endemic inconclusivity of all efforts to dissolve the intrinsic ambiguity of human action does not, however, justify abandoning the hope that eventually the 'philosopher's stone' of social science will be discovered, nor the analyses conducted on the assumption that such a hope is not vain.

Besides, Crespi's synthetic model contains features of its own that render it somewhat more interesting than other recently proposed models. Crespi blends the problematics of social action with the analysis of the ambivalent relation between action and the symbolic order, and with that of power, usefully expanding the scope of the latter to cover simultaneously, and in intimate interrelationship, the inner, 'subjective' capacity of the agent, the field of inter-agent engagements and the area of 'objective' constraints normally referred to as the 'social structure'. It is the reader's right to pass the final judgement on the degree to which such a shift in discursive practice has been theoretically successful and methodologically useful. Nevertheless, there is no doubt that Crespi's original approach will enrich the current sociological discourse and further broaden our understanding of the vast range of issues necessarily involved in its further progress.

ZYGMUNT BAUMAN

Author's Note

This is my own translation of my book *Azione Sociale e Potere* (Bologna: Il Mulino, 1989). Translations of extracts from non-English language texts have also been made by me.

In my examples I have used the pronoun 'he' in a generic sense solely in order to avoid the cumbersome repetition of 'he/she'.

Introduction

Since its origins sociology has been orientated to the application of *scientific* knowledge to human action and particularly to *social* action.

The idea of a rational knowledge of human action and its dominant passions was already present in Montaigne's *Essays*, in the *Treatise on Passions* by Descartes and in Pascal's *Pensées*. In the seventeenth century this knowledge was developed by moralists such as La Rochefoucault, La Bruyère, Shaftesbury and others. On the basis of this complex experience, during the time of the Enlightenment the project of a *science of man*, following the model of the sciences of nature, took shape.

Since the beginning natural science has been the main ideal reference for the science of man. This fact is responsible for what we may well consider as the paradox of the scientific knowledge of action: the removal of the specific character of human action itself. Kepler, Galilei and Newton founded the natural sciences on a mechanistic model whose physical laws could be translated in mathematical terms. The general conception of the world as a machine also drove the science of man to interpret moral and psychological phenomena as physical realities which could be empirically controlled. According to this perspective, man is considered as an *organism*, endowed with its own forces and functions in relation to the external environment, and the instinctual mechanisms which determine its behaviour are stressed. La Mettrie, assuming a critical attitude towards the metaphysical tradition, explicitly uses the concept of *homme machine*, of man as a mechanical apparatus, composed of different functions. It is true, however, that La Mettrie also mentions sensitive qualities and instincts, thus revealing an orientation which is in part different from Descartes's rigid mechanicism. On these presuppositions La Mettrie founds his conception of morality as the search for happiness, and conceives of the latter as 'an organic-materialistic type of existential well-being' (Moravia, 1982, p. 67).

Jeremy Bentham's utilitarian theory is also based on a similar conception. His theory is not only influenced by physical and biological models but also by Hume's critical thought and by the idea of social exchange and of economic utility proper to the optimistic image of the market expressed by Adam Smith.

Reducing the existential dynamic to the mere relationship between pleasure and pain, and defining utility as the minimization of pain and maximization of pleasure, Bentham's endeavour is orientated towards a 'moral algebra' based on the presupposition of the natural identity of an individual's interests. The idea that pain and pleasure, as well as utility, can be measured on the basis of intensity, duration, degree of predictability, connection between different forms of pleasure, number of individuals and so on, seems to guarantee the general criteria of an empirical code of politics and morality that can be verified by the same mathematical method. It is no coincidence that Bentham wished to become the 'Newton of moral sciences'.

This kind of approach tends to relate human action to the structure of natural needs and to a univocal criterion of utility, both for the individual and for society, in order to analyse action in the frame of attraction and repulsion of different instinctual drives and to measure it with the model of economic estimate.

The above-mentioned paradox is due to the fact that the more 'scientific' knowledge of action becomes, by reducing action to a physical phenomenon, the less the specific characteristics of human action are considered. The adoption of a univocal scientific model ends up by removing the object itself. This paradox characterizes the development of the utilitarian and positivistic theories of the last century and, as we shall see, it is still at work, although in different ways, even in some of the most recent sociological theories. However, it is also true that the problem raised by excessively reductivist physicalist and economicist theories, which influenced the first stage of the science of man, was perceived by sociology from the start.

Immediately after the French Revolution, the ideal of the Encyclopedists and Rousseau, of the total reform of man and society based on reason and pedagogy, was shaken. The impressive outburst of irrational forces during the Reign of Terror had shown that pedagogy, morality and philosophy were not sufficient to guarantee a rational development of social action. Since that time the perception has taken hold that the complexities of human behaviour should be studied not by the abstract reason of the *philosophes* but by empirical sciences.

It is in this context that Auguste Comte's project of a new positive science of social reality arises. Sociological science can no longer ignore the impact of the irrational or non-rational elements specific to human action: emotionalism, feelings, the need for religion and absolute beliefs can never again be considered as aspects to be controlled or eliminated through the development of reason, but must be taken into account in their specific forms and dealt with accordingly. With Comte, sociology finds its legitimation precisely in the fact that it is orientated to the analysis of those aspects neglected by economics and statistics.

Comte's positivism somehow shows the way to a scientific type of research, different from that dominant in the natural sciences, which led Dilthey and other German historicists to formulate the distinction between the sciences of nature (*Naturwissensschaften*) and the sciences of the spirit (*Geisteswissensschaften*). Aristotle observed that the problems of Beauty and Justice, to which 'political' science is dedicated, could not be treated with the same accuracy of logical-mathematical or physical sciences. Starting from an analogous consideration, Dilthey tries to preserve the objectivity of the historical and social sciences by the well-known distinction between *explanation* and *understanding*.

The critical experience of German historicism, which found its most mature expression in Max Weber, has remarkably enriched the analysis of social action by stressing the dimension of meaning. But, as we shall see, reference to the mathematical-natural sciences model is nevertheless still present even in Dilthey's notion of scientific knowledge. For a long time it reduced the possibilities opened up by the perception of the specific character of the social sciences. In contemporary sociology, besides the persistence of deterministic paradigms of a positivistic type, such as we can find in the different versions of neo-utilitarianism or sociobiology, there is still the tendency, even in theories influenced by phenomenology, existentialism and analytic philosophy, to eliminate the undetermined dimensions of subjectivity and consciousness. These theories tend to interpret action in terms of the observance of rules, language games and communicative structures, thus stressing the cultural dimension of action instead of those aspects more directly linked to life experience.

I do not intend to follow here the full historical itinerary of the theory of action. First, I shall attempt to criticize only some of the most meaningful positions of contemporary sociological theory of action in order to show their limitations. Then I shall suggest an alternative direction of research, through an appraisal of what I consider to be the most specific characteristics of the hermeneutical perspective, in order to develop a more adequate appreciation of the depth and complexity of social action. I believe that this approach is also the most useful for pointing to a new conception of subjectivity as well as to a new form of social projectuality.

1

In Search of Action

'We are not thinking decidedly enough about the essence of action.'
M. Heidegger

1.1 ACTION AND BEHAVIOUR

Before considering some of the contemporary sociological theories of social action, it is necessary to state briefly the meaning attributed here to the term *action*.

Through an anthropological analysis of the different manifestations of human action Arnold Gehlen has shown the remarkable deficiencies of man's, when compared with animals', *instinct*: 'poor in his sense faculties, lacking in his defence tools, naked, embryonic in his whole *habitus*, unsure in his instincts, man is the being which depends on action for his existence' (Gehlen, 1940, p. 11).

Establishing a distinction between *instincts*, that is, the endogenous and rigidly uniform stimuli of the organism, and *reactions of orientation*, that is, the highly differentiated responses activated by exogenous stimuli, Konrad Lorenz claimed that, whereas many animals are *also* capable of orientation reactions, man is *predominantly* characterized by them (cf. Poggi and Ryan, 1967, p. 366). These remarks can help us understand the difference between *behaviour* and *action*.

Behaviour refers to any kind of external movement of one or more living individuals in their own environment: the concept of behaviour allows us to understand the unity and coherence of these external manifestations without having to resort to some internal intentionality. In order to analyse and interpret behaviour it is sufficient to establish the connections between a given structure of the individual organism and the environment's structure, between the stimulus and the reaction to it:

survival instincts, the fulfilment of biological needs, the orientation towards reproduction and the survival of the species can represent in this case forms of adequate interpretation. According to this perspective we can apply the concept of behaviour to a molecule, to a plant, to an animal, and even to man when we can leave out of consideration his more specific qualities. Economics and statistics can well analyse the *average* behaviour of social actors in a particular environment. Action in its specific meaning can, on the contrary, be applied only to a man or a woman: a horse and a dog *behave* but they do not *act*.

That poverty and insecurity found by Gehlen in the human being's relation with instincts are at the origin of action. When we use the term action in its proper meaning, we must not only refer to the stimulus–reaction relation, but also consider the conscious or unconscious inner intentionality that is actually or potentially capable, at least up to a certain point, of autonomous choices. The concept of action thus implies the dimension of *intentionality*, even though its intensity or forms can be highly diversified: 'a man is the agent of an act if what he does can be described under an aspect that makes it intentional' (Davidson, 1980, p. 46; see also Searle, 1983).

The concept of intentionality, in the sense in which I use it here, should not be confused with *will*. The latter, so important in the Christian tradition, was ignored, as is well known, by the Greek philosophers and has been criticized by Nietzsche and several other contemporary philosophers, among whom we find Gilbert Ryle and Heidegger (see Arendt, 1978). Without entering into the problem here, let me just say that the concept of intentionality refers mainly to the fact that consciousness relates to objects and represents them, within the framework of its own life experience, through an interpretative elaboration of their meaning. Intentionality thus implies a relational and active dimension of consciousness which can find expression in the different forms of desire, choice, project and so on.

If today the analysis of action encounters some difficulties, this, as we shall see later, is due to the fact that the multiple dimensions of action tend to be ignored by the various contemporary theories of social action. The main reason for this deficiency is connected to the crisis of the idea of the subject and self-consciousness in our culture. I shall not rehearse the many aspects of this crisis here. Much has been written about it in recent years. I shall mention only one of its main causes: the difficulty of submitting subjectivity to the objectifications and measurements of scientific discourse. Subjectivity and self-consciousness as such are un-objectivable and unpredictable dimensions implying the unconditional aspect of liberty.

It is also true that the problem of the subject and self-consciousness has been considered in our cultural tradition by emphasizing the subject as substance and by attributing to it a stable *identity* which it is actually far from possessing. By considering self-consciousness as a transparent centre of cognition and conscious will, Descartes attributed to the subject the categories of his idea of rationality and ignored self-consciousness's manifold relations with the body, sensory faculties and emotions. In fact, Descartes's analyses of human passions considers these as somehow external to self-consciousness and his main attempt is to subordinate them to it (Barrett, 1986).

The critique by Nietzsche, Marx, Freud and Heidegger of the metaphysical conception of the subject and self-consciousness has undoubtedly increased the controversial recognition of the specificity of human action, but has not simply led, as some contemporary philosophers think, to the 'death of the subject'. If, on the one hand, there is no doubt that the traditional idea of subjectivity is obsolete, on the other hand, the very fact that one can speak of the death of the subject shows there is somebody who *speaks* about it and that 'somebody' cannot be anything else but a subject. In other words, the reference to subjectivity is implied in any discourse and cannot be easily eliminated. The fact that, with regard to the metaphysical tradition, the subject has somehow become much more mysterious, does not cancel the question of subjectivity. On the contrary, one is forced to pay constant attention to the different manifestations of individuality.

Heidegger's critique of the traditional concept of consciousness correctly stressed that consciousness does not have a founding function but arises in a situation where the *Dasein* is thrown from the beginning. The specific self-understanding of consciousness thus appears as essentially limited, constantly susceptible of error and self-deception and, in the final analysis, doomed to fail in its project of total transparency.

In this context self-consciousness can be essentially understood as a capacity to *negate* the objectivized forms. To be self-conscious does not mean knowing *who* we are, but knowing who we are *not*: it is characteristic of the ego to differentiate itself not only from external things but also from the internal objectifications that constitute its own Self or *identity*.

George Mead's and Sartre's respective analyses of the process through which the Self is constructed show that both the dimension of *identification* (and interiorization) with and *differentiation* from the other are equally important for the development of self-consciousness (see Aboulafia, 1986). *Identity* thus appears only as part of self-consciousness, the latter also always including the capacity to differentiate from any form of determinacy, or what we could call the capacity of non-identity.

'Man is the being who can say *no*' (Scheler, 1927): the potentiality of negation and differentiation is at the basis of that essential insecurity and weakness of the human being stressed by Gehlen. Self-consciousness produces a reflexivity that breaks the *immediacy*, the simple accord of the living individual with himself, thus creating an irretrievable gap between the individual and his instinctual drives: at this point a new settlement based on *symbolic mediation* becomes necessary. What before was lived through the immediacy of an instinctual response has now to be elaborated by a system of symbolic meanings, that is, by those expressive and normative forms the sociologists call *culture*. The instinctual mechanism is thus substituted by representations, values, rules, orientating the action of the individual as well as that of collectivities.

It was Gehlen again who showed how culture institutionalizes some meanings and aims of action through codified forms which lighten (*entlasten*) the burden of the self-conscious individual, who otherwise would have to rediscover each time what to do in any given situation (Gehlen, 1940).

As we shall see later, there are two major conditions which characterize the dimension of action: the first is connected with the breaking of the direct relation between behaviour and its meaning, a relation specific to the animal world. Action always has a symbolic meaning related to the inner world of the actor, a meaning that cannot be taken for granted once and for all, but has to be verified every time. When an animal eats, it is certainly satisfying a biological need; but when a man eats he may also do it as a ritual, as an expression of his social position, or for psychological reasons connected with insecurity, aggressiveness and so on.

The second condition concerns the constant oscillation between the need for *determinacy* (the social predictability necessary for social life, the reinforcement of identity both at the individual and collective level) and the *indeterminacy* due to the complexity of life experience and its necessary adaptation to the ever-changing material or cultural conditions of the natural and social environment. Being determinate, the forms of symbolic mediation in fact always serve to reduce the complexity of action and, in the final analysis, always turn out to be inadequate for the different needs that emerge in life experience (see Crespi, 1982, 1985). Both these conditions will be more widely analysed later.

1.2 ACTION AND SOCIAL SYSTEM

In the first phase of its development social theory was characterized by the attempt to reduce action to behaviour and the consideration of action mainly to 'doing something' (Arendt, 1958). The notion of purposive action, or action orientated to manipulation and production, has been predominant over that of action as the expression of existential meanings, values and subjective feelings. The subjective dimension of action produces a high degree of complexity for empirical research: we can expect from the individual what is most 'unlikely' and unpredictable, and it is precisely this aspect which creates the greatest difficulties for a *science* of action.

The two main theoretical approaches that in our tradition have tried to reduce the complexity of action are utilitarianism and behaviourism. Both these theories tend to analyse social action within deterministic frames of reference, overlooking what Parsons called the *voluntaristic* dimension of action.

With regard to the problem of the manifold meanings of human action, utilitarianism finds itself in an *impasse* or *dead end* situation: the more the utilitarian model tries to be specific and effective by guaranteeing predictability and concreteness of results, the more it must reduce the analysed phenomena to the point of excessive abstraction.

The tendency of utilitarian theories to relate any kind of action to a stable structure of natural needs shared by all social actors, undervalues the cultural dimension which, through the interiorization of values and patterns of behaviour, determines the socialization of individuals and the deep orientation of their life experience. Whereas for economic science the selection of only a few statistically relevant aspects of the strategies inspired by interests is legitimate, for sociology this selection implies the risk of overlooking the variety of symbolic meanings that orientate social action, even in organizations which are more directly linked with economic interests. In this case the different 'logics' of both individual and collective action, as well as the contradictions characteristic of any social system, are no longer apparent. When utilitarianism stands by its presuppositions, it shows, as Bernard Williams remarked, a strong tendency to oversimplification and it appears glaringly inadequate to deal with the real world (see Smart and Williams, 1973).

The more contemporary authors who use the utilitarian approach are aware that it is necessary to give space to the dimension of meaning and cultural values as well as to the many ways in which action finds its expression, the less different their approach seems from other more comprehensive theoretical frames of reference. Today – and this is another aspect of the aforementioned dead end – the utilitarian model seems to oscillate between the tendency, on the one hand, to interpret action within rigidly deterministic patterns based on the structure of natural needs and the material conditions of the social situation, and, on the other hand, to widen its analytical frame by including more complex dimensions.

The empirical specificity of this approach seems to be strictly linked to the evaluation of action in terms of profits and losses, as well as to the principle of maximization of pleasure and the possibility of identifying invariant relations between behavioural reactions and objective conditions of social situations. But when the utilitarian model also tries to include wider psychological and cultural dimensions it loses its identity and becomes more and more like other theoretical approaches, such as functionalism, systemic or even phenomenological theory.

I shall not deal here with the behaviouristic approach which is even more reductive, since it explicitly avoids any reference to the inner intentionality of action. The stimulus–response scheme, developed by analogy with the animal world, is totally inadequate to represent the multidimensional reality of social dynamics.

In contemporary sociology the most ambitious attempt to develop a general theory of action in a wider perspective than that of positivistic theories was made, as is well known, by Talcott Parsons. His critique of utilitarianism and behaviourism stresses their inadequacy. By defining his theory as 'voluntaristic', Parsons seeks to avoid two extremes: on the one hand, the *materialistic* or radical positivistic theory, which considers action as the result of hereditary and environmental conditions, and, on the other hand, the *idealistic* theory, which considers action only as the free expression of the individual.

Parsons thinks that utilitarianism, which underrates the impact of values and social norms, excessively emphasizes the rational criterion of efficiency. According to Parsons, four elements characterize utilitarianism: *atomism*, namely, 'the strong tendency to consider mainly the properties of conceptually isolated unit acts and to infer the properties of systems of action only by a process of "direct" generalization from these'; the concept of *rationality*, namely, the 'right' selection of appropriate means to ends; *empiricism*, in its most naïve form; *randomness of ends*, without any consideration of the relations of ends to each other (Parsons, 1973, pp. 52–60). The reductive rationalist model of utilitarianism also overlooks other forms of action, for instance the 'ritual' ones, which are often relevant in social life (see Parsons, 1973, p. 57).

Parsons rightly stresses the connection between this conception of rationality and 'the prominence of science in the climate of opinion of the time'. Action is in fact analysed 'in terms of the analogy between the scientific investigator and the actor in ordinary practical activities' (Parsons, 1937, p. 58). Scientific knowledge thus becomes the only type of meaningful orientation in the system of action. In this context the ends of action appear to be linked to the contingent situation, and there is no possibility of conceiving of them as meaningful in themselves and relatively independent from the given situation.

In the positivistic perspective, the only possible criterion is to ground the choices of action on the scientific knowledge of empirical reality, but, as Parsons observes, in this case action is entirely determined by its conditions. Without the independence of ends, the distinction between conditions and means becomes meaningless: action is thus perceived as 'a process of rational adaptation to these conditions'. Positivistic thought is caught in what Parsons calls the 'utilitarian dilemma': 'either the active agency of the actor in the choice of ends is an independent factor in action' or the ends 'are assimilated to the conditions of the situation' (Parsons, 1937, p. 64).

Referring to Durkheim, Parsons rightly stresses the fact that the decisions of the actor are always orientated not only by interests but also by values, and thus defines action as a tension between the normative order and the conditions of the situation.

Parsons's concept of 'voluntaristic' action is, at least potentially, open to the possibility of considering the negative capacity of consciousness in its relation to objectivation and thus of recognizing the relative autonomy of the social actor from the situation. Moreover, the reference to values yields an acknowledgement of the plurality of the orientations of action, by showing that the latter cannot be interpreted within a univocal frame of reference.

However, difficulties arise when Parsons, from the analysis of the unity of action, starts to consider the problem of social order and the relation between action and social system. As he has no means of relating the actor's situation to any existential category, Parsons cannot consider the different levels of action and cannot establish the genetic process of the cultural forms.

The values considered by Parsons are always already *there*, in their connection with structures and functional requirements of the system: he has no means by which to consider values also as the product of an intersubjective process of communication, connected with the original requirements of constructing meaning, establishing identity and founding normative predictability. The result is that, after *The Structure of Social Action*, in *Toward a General Theory of Action* and *The Social System* Parsons tends to give increasing importance to the problem of the functioning of the social system as such, and to aspects connected with the maintenance of social order.

Following Durkheim, Parsons considers the problem of order in terms of the social actors' interiorization of values functional to the maintenance of the social system, and in terms of control of deviant behaviours. However, Parsons does not develop the possibilities implied in the acknowledgement of the importance of values in order to understand social action. This is due to the lack of an adequate theory of the genesis of culture, which would take into account the creative character of action consequent on the capacity of subjective consciousness to negate the objectivated forms, transform them or even substitute them with other determined forms of symbolic-normative mediation. In the final analysis, action thus becomes for Parsons merely an undifferentiated energy which has to be orientated by values and behavioural patterns in order to obtain performances functional to the social system. Even if in relation to the social system actors not only represent a source of performances but also of requests, they are mainly considered in terms of their status-role within the system, or as 'abstract holders of a position' (Habermas, 1987).

As Habermas has remarked, the problems of the *functional* integration of the social system (allocation and mobilization of resources) become dominant over the problems of *social* integration (cultural tradition, socialization, solidarity), and in the end integration is considered only in terms of a functional prerequisite of the system. In this context the cultural system loses its own autonomy in relation to the social system and becomes a mere function supplying forms for the definition of collective goals, values and motivations, techniques, educational methods, norms and so on. Even if it is true that culture performs all these functions, it is also true that Parsons, by stressing the dimension of integration, forgets the active aspect of the process of meaning production, in terms of a critique of the prevailing orders and a factor of change and innovation, which depends not only on the prerequisites of the system as such but also on the practical experience of the social actors, at both the individual and the collective level.

With Parsons, as with Durkheim, the individual appears as a tendentially centrifugal force which has to be orientated and eventually compelled, by gratifications and punishments, in order to guarantee the fulfilment of the social system's requirements. In this perspective integration is always positive: the ambivalence of the forms of determination of individual or collective identity and of norms is not considered. That ambivalence is in fact due to the reductive character of any form of determination as such: while determination is necessary to establish identity and social order, precisely because it is determined it is also always, in the final analysis, inadequate to the complexity of life experience. Hence the fact that the forms of determination are also always a cause of contradictions, inequality and conflictual tensions, and sometimes even of social destruction.

In the relation between action and the forms of symbolic-normative mediation, the first is not the only source of disorder, when the forms of mediation do not succeed in controlling it; also the forms of mediation themselves, because of their reductive character, can produce disorder. On the other hand, the action of the individual is not only a potential cause of indeterminacy but, due to the need of identity and of reciprocal recognition among social actors, it is also at the origin of the production of determinacy and predictability functional to social order.

The absence of a morphogenetic approach to the relation between action and culture prevents Parsons's theory from giving adequate consideration to the contradictory requirements of determinacy and indeterminacy which characterize that relation: when only the systemic dimension is emphasized, the multiple dimensions of action tend to disappear.

The reductive character of the functional approach was brought to its conclusion by Niklas Luhmann, who entirely eliminates the tension between action and social system which Parsons, as mentioned above, had initially indicated as a specific dimension of the theory of action. For Luhmann the individual is no more a constitutive element of social reality but is only the product of the functional principle of complexity reduction which regulates the maintenance of the social system. Action thus appears only as a 'selection' of the system itself.

As I have already said elsewhere (Crespi, 1985), the concept of complexity reduction which forms the basis of Luhmann's theory implies reference to an active principle of selection, which can be understood only as the negative capacity of consciousness in its relation to objectivated forms. Luhmann, even though he recognizes the importance of negation in the concept of complexity reduction, does not relate the latter to subjectivity but to the social system itself, thus attributing to the system a quality that can only be specific of an individual.

If Parsons's systemic paradigm is, as we have said, devoid of any consideration of the morphogenetic processes through which a social system comes into existence, Luhmann accentuates the rejection of any reference to categories not already included in his self-referential systemic model. The fact that contemporary systemic theory is somewhat closed to every dimension external to the established system offers good grounds for Habermas's critique, which understands Luhmann's systemic theory as a social technology based on the implicit identification of the social scientist with the praxis typical of the system he is investigating (Habermas and Luhmann, 1971).

1.3 RATIONALITY AND THE THEORY OF ACTION

Keeping their distance from functionalism, some contemporary sociological theories, referring to the tradition of utilitarian individualism, have stressed both the subjective and the rational dimensions. On the one hand, the critique of the individualistic approach, by those who have stressed the dependence of action on the structural and material conditions, has considered the attribution of rationality to action as the social scientist's *ex-post* 'rationalization' of behaviours which are actually the product of those conditions. On the other hand, those who only wished to emphasize the subjective dimension have stressed the irrational and emotional elements of human action, considering it mainly as the product of unconscious drives. But perhaps the strongest critique of the rationalist theories connected to the methodological individualism of von Mises, von Hayek and Popper, has been made by those who, referring to the analytical philosophy of language and to the concept of 'following a rule', have emphasized that action depends not on the motivations of the actor but on the latent and manifest rules, on the predominant values, representations and codified patterns of behaviour which, once interiorized, orientate the social actors in a more or less conscious way.

The authors who have tried to advocate the rational model of action have generally reacted to these different criticisms by recognizing the necessity of widening the concept of rationality itself. This has led to an attempt to integrate the utilitarian model or that of purposive rationality by referring to the manifold meanings and values which orientate action, and by assuming that there are many different *reasons* of action.

Without going into a debate that, starting from Max Weber, has run throughout the entire sociological discourse and has also involved the economic and juridical theories, I shall only discuss here the possibility of maintaining the 'rational' model of action, even if integrated in the above-mentioned sense. The question is whether the attempt to broaden the concept of rationality leads to such contradictions as to make the model obsolete. There is no doubt that rationality as a general frame of reference allows us to analyse action both as an 'objective' reality and as an expression of the individual. The possibility of developing a science of subjective elements, instead of giving way to a deterministic model such as we find in the different forms of structuralism, is seemingly obtained through the equation between individuality and rationality. In fact, if individuals follow a universal rational pattern, their action can be analysed in terms of the objective connections between intended ends and the procedures adequate to reach them. The possibility of interpreting action as the product of *calculus* seems to lead to a sort of mathematics of action, undoubtedly considered 'scientific' by the prevailing epistemological criteria. The individualistic principle is saved by the fact that it is the individual who evaluates the situation and makes decisions between concrete alternatives; while reference to his rational standards saves the objectivistic principle. Thus apparently the rational theory of action seems to find a perfect solution, avoiding the risks of both extreme subjectivism and determinism: hence the success of the theory.

But if we consider it more attentively, it appears that the idea of the rationality of action is based on an anthropological conception which interprets human action as the product of a structure of natural needs.

Marshall Sahlins has recently made a critique of the entire empirical epistemology which, following the tradition of the Enlightenment, is at the basis of Western culture. The anthropological perspective that from the beginning has orientated the social sciences was founded on the concept of the individual as a centre of needs in relation to objects able to give pleasure or pain, in a situation of scarcity. It is in this context that the instrumental and functional conception of *Homo oeconomicus occidentalis*, which interprets society in terms of a *market*, has gained ground.

Referring to the distinction between natural need and cultural form, Sahlins recalls that hunger can be considered an *animal necessity*, which as such is not yet a *human need*. In fact, the organic necessity of food is, on the one hand, connected to a chemical system (proteins, calories and so on) and, on the other hand, it can be interpreted in terms of the limits of survival of the body. But in man, hunger as such does not presuppose a definite object nor a mental status nor a specific action. On the contrary, every human need for food is already a cultural determination of the nourishing object and it is connected to a social consciousness of it. An analogous argument could be made for the sexual drive (see Sahlins, 1986).

In this perspective a culture different from ours, not based on the needs of the individual or on the imperative of their reward as an uncontroversial *a priori* of society, could well consider society itself as an *a priori* and as the normal conditioning of the individual's needs. In this case an insatiable appetite, instead of being considered, as in our tradition, the natural basis of society, could be seen as a pathological manifestation of social action. As an example of this Sahlins refers to the

'Windigo psychosis' of the Canadian Indians, as it was described by the Jesuit missionaries of the seventeenth century.

The Canadian Indians considered needs not as the natural basis of social life but as what in fact they are, namely a *social construction*. In this context even hunger was for them a social relation. This explains why the hunting spoils were equally distributed among all members of the tribe and why, even in situations of extreme scarcity, instead of being hoarded they were entirely eaten, with no worry about the future. Mixing an habitual generosity with an equally habitual stoicism, this particular culture, which put no curbs on sexual drives, to the astonishment of the good priests, severely controlled the pangs of hunger that were considered to be dangerous elements threatening disintegration of the social unit.

This shows, according to Sahlins, that what the Canadian Indians' society considered as folly (that is, the insatiable need of food), became in Western culture the ground for economic rationality, precisely during the period when other *different* cultures were discovered. The theoretical framework for this notion of rationality located the origin of society in the search for individual profit to the detriment of the interests of others: 'one society's madness may be another's economics' (Sahlins, 1986).

Sahlins' analysis, which I have summarized very roughly here, is a good example of the peculiar arbitrariness of any attempt to identify a univocal relationship between a natural structure and a form of action. The biological structure is, in the human world, in fact always symbolically mediated, and the meanings of action are always to be referred to the sociocultural context and to the life experience of the social actors: what is important is not the identification of the 'natural' needs but the knowledge of the given *interpretations* of them.

Some non-utilitarian theories of needs can be recalled here (see Marcuse, 1955; Heller, 1974). However, as I have already said, in our tradition there is a strong link between the positivistic model of the natural sciences and the tendency to stress the structure of natural needs, which maintains that the social actor is led by objective forces of attraction and repulsion.

If, on the one hand, cultural anthropology has made a great contribution by stressing the importance of social rules and cultural values in establishing the prevailing criteria of rationality, the development of cognitive psychology and of psychoanalysis has also provided support for the critique of *Homo oeconomicus* model, by showing the limitations of the analysis of economic strategies and *ex-post* rationalization forms, and by stressing the symbolic meanings that interfere in the estimate of profits and losses. Game theory, as well as the recent developments of rational choice theory, has also shown the impact of the relational dimension on the evaluation of such profits and losses. This is where the tendency, shown by various authors who still refer to the utilitarian model, of widening the concept of rationality originates.

In this perspective I shall briefly consider here two different types of theory: the first, more directly connected to behaviourism, is the well-known theory of social exchange formulated by George Homans; the second, more clearly related to individualism, has been recently developed by Raymond Boudon. I shall then consider the recent positions of Jeffrey Alexander and Luciano Gallino. In his book *Social Behaviour – Its Elementary Forms* (1961), George Homans has tried to analyse social behaviour within a general frame of reference based on a set of empirical propositions derived from behavioural psychology and elementary economics. Here too behaviour was envisaged as 'a function of its payoff: in amount and kind it depends on the amount and kind of reward and punishment it fetches' (Homans, 1961, p. 13). Homans explicitly refers to the behavioural patterns developed by Skinner in his studies of animal behaviour.

In this latter context, action is interpreted in relation to the frequency of a concrete activity, to the punishment–reward status of the organism, to the number of stimuli, and to the negative or positive reinforcements of an activity. However, in the case of human action Homans recognized the necessity to introduce other variables related to the complexity of the learning process and the type of relations that the individual establishes with his past experiences. When compared to animal behaviour, this involves a much greater differentiation of the activities which an individual can develop in relation to a concrete stimulus.

Homans pays particular attention to two kinds of variable: *values* and *quantity* of action; that is, the meaning attributed to an action by the actor and its variations in time, on the one hand, and, on the other, the frequency of the same action in relation both to values and to the time dimension, as well as to the degree of reward actually obtained.

In this perspective Homans had to recognize that the evaluation of the cost–profit relation of an action is remarkably difficult to explain and predict if, following the ideal type of value-orientated rational action formulated by Weber, we take into account the fact that there are values, such as the moral or aesthetic ones, which are in themselves their own reward. In any case, one must refer to the values interiorized by the individual as a result of his past experiences in relation to his sociocultural context, to his or her feelings, to the norms and institutionalized forms of social exchange specific to that context, and so on. The difficulty, as Homans himself observed, comes from the fact that the more those variables are to be taken into account, the more the complexity of the unity of action emerges.

Homans's attempt is a good example of the above-mentioned *empasse* of the utilitarian model: in order to create an objective frame of reference for the interpretation of action, one must give a specific character to the concept of rationality, thus reducing as much as possible the variables to which reference is made. But precisely because it is sensible to the empirical reality of action, the same rational theory tends to take into account values, norms, meanings, institutionalized structures and so on, thus losing the specificity of the rational profit–loss model. If, as Homans says, 'the new economic man is plain man' (Homans, 1961, p. 80), then the concept of economy itself becomes excessively wide and indeterminate. This is a contradiction common to all attempts to base the interpretation of social action on a strictly rationalistic pattern.

Analogous difficulties have been met by Raymond Boudon in his effort to construct a rational model of social action, taking into account as much as possible the plurality of elements involved in action processes.

I shall not go through the entire output of this important author, who has progressively revised his initial rigid neo-positivistic position: I shall only refer here to a recent text by Boudon (1987), where he reconsiders, with new integrations, aspects he had analysed previously (Boudon, 1977, 1984).

Boudon makes a distinction between the two images of *Homo sociologicus* prevalent in contemporary sociology: the first, with which he sympathizes, is of a *rational* type and is founded on the general principle that in order to explain the actions, attitudes and beliefs of a social actor, one must prove that, considering his *past*, his *resources* and his *environment*, he had *good reasons* to take those actions, to assume those attitudes or those beliefs (see Boudon, 1987, p. 175).

The utilitarian concept of rationality as *rational choice* is widened by Boudon by reference to the relational model of game theory and to Simon's concept of limited rationality: it aims at getting beyond the Weberian *teleological* model (performative rationality) as well as the *assiological* model (value-orientated rationality). The concept of *good reasons* is intended to overcome the univocal concept of rationality of the utilitarian tradition, but cannot be simply identified, says Boudon, with the Weberian ideal types of rationality.

The second image of *Homo sociologicus* is the *irrational* one. This model explains action, not by the reasons given by the actor himself but in relation to the psychological, cultural and structural *causes* which determined it. Boudon's critique against the oversimplifications of the 'irrational' model are often very much to the point, but for our purpose it is the concept of *good reasons* that must be challenged. Using several examples, Boudon seeks to prove that actions considered irrational by the observer's criteria are in fact rational once their relation with the sociocultural context, values, limits of knowledge, and real interests of the social actors is perceived. In this perspective Boudon introduces two new dimensions of the concept of rationality: the first is *rationality of position* (*rationalité de position*), that is, rationality linked to the 'immediate experience' of the specific situation by the actor; the second is *rationality of disposition* (*rationalité de disposition*), an explanation of the differences of their action by reference to the unequal cognitive resources of the social actors.

Boudon's dispositions are not to be conceived of as forces determining the social actor, but as '*données internes*', or inner conditions, which, together with the '*données externes*', or external conditions, form the basis of the individual action. Boudon thus recognizes that there are many different types of rationality: hence he believes he has developed a frame of reference broader than the utilitarianist and the Weberian ideal types, while avoiding at the same time the inconveniences of the 'irrational' model.

Recalling the critique already made of Homans's approach, the question is whether the assumption of different kinds of *good reasons* (teleological, assiological, positional and dispositional) maintains the specific characteristics of a *rational* model, so that the new aspects can be seen as an extension of that model, or whether, as I believe, the recognition of the new dimensions explodes the entire model, leading to a completely different approach.

If all the different variables included in the concept of *good reasons* are taken into account (environment, sociocultural context, values, psychological situation, cognitive resources and so on) the concept of rationality appears to lose all specificity and is reduced to the mere recognition that any action has some *sense*. Boudon in fact explicitly acknowledges the importance of meaning and, referring to Weber, holds that there are actions – for example, those dictated by indignation – which cannot be analysed in utilitarian terms. In this case the concept of *good reasons* does not correspond to the idea of rationality as the explanation of action in terms of intentional orientation towards specific aims or rewards. But once this concept of rationality is abandoned, we are definitely out of the 'rationalistic' utilitarian tradition and we have to deal with a wide concept of meaning which can only be analysed, as I shall try to show later, in a phenomenological and hermeneutical perspective.

A somewhat similar critique can be made of two new approaches to the problem of action: those of Jeffrey Alexander and Luciano Gallino. I shall consider both proposals very briefly as examples of the attempt to widen the rationalistic frame of reference.

In order to establish the fundamental criteria for a general theoretical logic in sociological thought, Jeffrey Alexander formulates a *multidimensional* approach for the analysis of social action which, together with the concept of social order, he considers an essential element of sociological theory (see Alexander, 1982).

Alexander, like Parsons, criticizes the tendency to interpret action within a *unidimensional* frame of reference, both with the *instrumentally rational* type of approach, which analyses action only in terms of adaptation to external conditions in a means–ends calculative perspective, or with the *non-rational normative* type of approach, which considers action only in terms of subjectivity, voluntarism and freedom. Both the objectivistic–deterministic approach of utilitarianism and of behaviourism, and the subjectivistic–constructivist approach (Mead, Schütz) are, according to Alexander, the product of a dichotomy repeating the eternal opposition between materialism and idealism. The *multidimensional* approach should instead take into account at the same time the rational instrumental dimension and the non-rational normative dimension of action, the internal voluntaristic dimension of subjectivity and the external objective conditions, free will as well as coercion. On the one hand, Alexander criticizes the different theoretical attempts 'to raise to the most generalized theoretical level conceptions of rationality that are actually grounded at more specific empirically oriented levels of analysis' (Alexander, 1982, p. 85). Schütz's reference to rationality as 'common sense' derives, according to Alexander, 'not from a conception of the basic, presuppositional alternatives of action, but from his more detailed empirical reconstruction of the cultural components of common sense as one of the principal "phenomenological worlds" that compose reality' (Alexander, 1982, p. 86). Similarly the anthropological debate over the nature of symbolic action (Levi Bruhl, Evans Pritchard) refers to causal propositions about the interrelation between ritual and social structure. Freud grounds his concept of rationality on empirical notions of health and illness, while Weber's distinction between rational and non-rational action builds on his empirical theory about the direction of historical change (see Alexander, 1982, p. 86).

On the other hand, Alexander criticizes the approaches which relate rationality to the normative criterion of scientific rationality (Jarvie, Agassi, Pareto), or to 'substantive rationality' (Weber, Mannheim, Marcuse, Habermas). According to Alexander, these criteria transform ideological elements connected to specific forms of rationality (scientific, ethical-humanistic) into general theoretical presuppositions.

Alexander believes that every social theory 'must evaluate action in terms of some standard of scientific accuracy and in terms of some substantive moral goal', but he also believes that the possibility of making such ideal judgements 'depends on the prior existence of a certain more general orientation' (Alexander, 1982, p. 89). This general orientation would be provided, according to Alexander, by the connection between action and social order, the latter being defined as the problem of how 'individual units, of whatever motivation, are arranged in nonrandom social patterns' (ibid., p. 92).

Alexander thinks that a connection between order and free will is possible: in the scientific analysis of social action we can in fact predict actions that will frequently occur, without thus implying that they result from a strict determinism. The *multidimensional* approach should offer a non-reductive frame of reference, avoiding the unidimensional approaches of both objective determinism and subjective idealism. At the most general presuppositional level, voluntarism can be considered as a structural or 'formal' property of action, while order appears at the same time as an *external* (coercion) and *internal* (interiorization of norms) dimension: accepting voluntarism does not necessarily mean denying coercion, nor does recognizing the latter deny voluntarism.

While Alexander has correctly stressed the reductive character of the different theoretical approaches about action, the way in which he tries to connect the opposed perspectives in a multidimensional frame of reference appears inadequate to establish a *theory* of action. His proposal can be considered rather as a taxonomy of the different elements that are to be taken into account and of the questions that must be solved by a theory of action. Recognizing, as Alexander does, that it is impossible to exhaust neither the dimension of action in the problem of social order nor the dimension of order in that of the constructive spontaneity of action, amounts to recognizing the fundamental contradictory character of the social situation as such. One has then to explain this irreconcilable condition with a general theory of action showing the specific relation between action and its existential and social conditions, as well as between action and the forms of symbolic mediation. In this perspective, as we shall see later, it is possible to stress at the same time the *necessity* of determinate normative forms founding social predictability and the *limits* of these same forms as such, for, being determinate, they are always reductive of the indeterminate complexity of life experience. In the absence of a more developed theoretical conceptualization, the orientation to a broader frame of reference risks being nothing more than an expression of good intentions.

An attempt towards broadening the instrumentally rational approach has also been made by Luciano Gallino in his book *L'attore sociale* (The Social Actor, 1987). Gallino adopts a strong concept of the actor as 'an autonomous individual capable of maintaining and reproducing himself, by use of the most diverse elements, as, for instance, the successive forms of individualization offered by social roles which are often inconsistent and unrelated' (Gallino, 1987, p. 176).

By stressing the autonomy of the actor in his relation to the different conditions of the natural environment and the social system, Gallino believes in the 'intrinsic superiority' for sociological analysis of the theory of the *actor* compared with the theory of *action* (Parsons, Boudon). In what appears to me a rather controversial distinction, Gallino considers the theory of action as limited to a 'field theory' where, for example, the relation between class differences and behaviour should be analysed, while the theory of the actor should refer to the individual as 'a self-organized, self-preserving and self-reproductive unit, different from the systemic unit of which he is a constitutive element' (Gallino, 1987, p. 14).

Gallino criticizes both Husserl's phenomenological approach and Schütz's sociological theory, because they tend to stress the pre-predicative character of *Lebenswelt* (Lifeworld) as a 'common sense' structure prior to individual action. A theory of the actor, according to Gallino, should be 'predicative', that is, it should refer to the specific uniqueness of the individual. A theory of the actor must explain 'why individuals who participate in a common lifeworld do act in many different ways, establishing conflictual relations among themselves' (Gallino, 1987, p. 13).

If Gallino is right to stress the relative autonomy of the actor in his relation to the natural and social conditions, the frame of reference which he tries to develop from the above-mentioned presuppositions is open to many criticisms. Gallino builds up his conception of the actor by referring to sociobiology, cognitive psychology, psychoanalysis, the analysis of artificial intelligence and systemic theory. He himself recognizes that his *telefunctional model* is 'highly syncretic' as within it

> the computational paradigm is applied in accordance with the criteria of cognitivism; the processes of imagination and thought are derived from psychoanalysis, while the different sub-systems are connected to the functional requirements of a mental system, which, being the product of bio-cultural evolution, is intrinsically oriented to pursuing, through the most rewarding biological and symbolical forms, the ultimate ends of survival, self-maintenance and reproduction. (Gallino, 1987, p. 56)

I cannot go here into the analysis of the various components of Gallino's theory of the actor, but I must observe that the high degree of complexity of the telefunctional model seems to make its empirical application extremely difficult. In fact, the validity of the examples of empirical analysis developed in Gallino's book seems to be grounded, not so much on the telefunctional model itself, but mainly on the interpretation of the processes of individualization and identification connected with the fundamental need of the social actor to be reassured about his own identity in his relation with other actors.

The interpretative categories used by this author thus seem to be based on some general presuppositions about the existential situation of the individual as such. But these presuppositions are not adequately developed in the telefunctional frame of reference which, in fact, despite its manifold structure, in its reference to the 'most rewarding solution' and to the ultimate aims of survival, self-maintenance and self-reproduction, still appears very much dependent on a more simplistic utilitarian conception of rationality.

Gallino's attempt at broadening the rationality frame of reference does not take into account all the theoretical implications consequent on the recognition of the existential and symbolical dimensions of action.

1.4 ACTION AND LABOUR

In his book *La Sociologie de l'action* (The Sociology of Action) Alain Touraine (1965) assumes an equally critical attitude towards both the functionalistic and the 'idealistic' approach: 'the sense of an action can neither be reduced to the adaptation of the actor to a more or less institutionalised normative system, nor to the expression of the mind through a social activity' (Touraine, 1965, p. 9).

Touraine maintains, in opposition to Parsons, that a sociological theory should explain the origin of the values that orientate action. This origin is not to be found in a meta-social principle but in action itself, even if the latter does generally create values 'neither consciously nor by free will': the task of the sociology of action is to discover the reasons which determine the development of certain values.

According to Touraine, the concept which is open to an adequate understanding of the relation between nature and culture and gives to human action its specific character is *labour*. Touraine, following Marx, defines labour as an 'action related to the non-social world' and as 'a principle of transformation of man and nature' (Touraine, 1965, p. 10). Action, however, cannot be considered apart from the meaning that it has for the actor. Touraine rejects the materialist deterministic approach: it is impossible to explain social action as a result of the internal logic of the technological process or the economic system. On the one hand, technological and economic activities appear in fact as the product of a complex decision-making process: 'Property seems less important than power and social action should be interpreted, through the social relations and the cultural orientations, in its own terms' (Touraine, 1965, p. 13). On the other hand, even if the social meaning of an action is not to be identified with the meaning attributed to it by the actor, the fact that an action is related to the intentional meaning of the individual cannot simply lead to an interpretation of action in terms of the laws of the historical process (see Touraine, 1965, p. 26).

Touraine's attempt is particularly challenging, as the analysis of action according to its *own* sense implies that it can neither be derived from material conditions, nor identified with a transcendental meaning of history, nor even entirely referred to individual psychology. The question lies in the adequacy of the concept of *labour*, as Touraine uses it, for defining the specific level of social action and interpreting the relation between the latter and the actor.

Touraine observes that Weber's experience has shown the limitations of getting at historical data only through the two-fold filter of the orientations of both the actor and the social scientist. In this case social action is interpreted mainly with reference to the ideal types formulated through historical analysis. Action appears thus merely as the reflex of the system of meanings and of their inner coherence, while social conditions are simply added to the value orientations without being considered as constitutive elements of the social process.

If on the one hand Touraine refers to Weberian ideal types to avoid the reification intrinsic to the concept of *historical factors*, on the other hand he criticizes them as inadequate to represent the concrete level of historical situations and social relations. According to Touraine, action must be interpreted not only as the product of value orientations but also as an active dimension creating values and orientations. For the same reasons, although recognizing the importance of the functional approach for the analysis of the *forms* of 'sociability', Touraine criticizes Talcott Parsons and stresses the constitutive character of action for the social system.

For Touraine, the concept of labour is the most apt for taking into account the creative character of action: 'To the extent that action is creator of culture, the analysis should start neither from the natural and contradictory condition of the individual, nor from the conditions of the collective action, but from the action that creates history, that is from labour' (Touraine, 1965, pp. 91–2). In Touraine's perspective, labour becomes historical action as such: a specific human activity which transforms not only the material environment where the individual acts but also the social group and, in the last analysis, the entire society. Through labour activities the individual and the group become conscious of their being as historical actors, that is, as 'creators of a certain change'. With the concept of labour, the theory of action overcomes the difficulty of choice between the value and the deterministic approach, labour being at the same time a relation with the material conditions and an activity transforming the latter, as well as a source of values. Labour is at the same time action and situation, or a self-regualted *praxis*.

As a relation between the mind and its object, Touraine's notion of labour has to be understood in the traditional dialectic scheme and appears to be connected to the concept of *historical subject*. Touraine's conception of the latter aptly refers to society as 'collective labourer', namely, the capacity of society to consider its environment as the product of its own activity; this capacity is strictly connected with *technological* development, as a kind of labour which masters its own instruments and results.

The historical subject bears no correspondence with the individual, but must be thought of in terms of 'the interpretation of the historical situation as a whole, as the meaning of a certain collective experience and, moreover, as a way of defining and organizing a certain field of work' (Touraine, 1965, p. 39).

On the basis of the concepts of labour and historical subject, Touraine distinguishes three analytical levels of the social phenomenon: (a) the *actionalist* level, which studies in particular the historical subject and its action as ground for the normative orientations of social action; (b) the *functionalist* level which analyses social forms and systems within which action is organized; (c) the *structuralist* level which considers the symbolic forms expressed in action, also used by the social systems. Functionalism and structuralism thus seem to be complementary in Touraine's actionalist approach.

Three main *themes* or 'types of orientation of social action' correspond to these three levels. The first theme is constituted by the relation between social actor and nature, defined by Touraine as 'historical consciousness or labour'; the second, 'sociability', considers the relation of the social actor with other members of society; the third analyses the contradictions between nature and culture and is defined as 'existential or anthropological consciousness'. These three fundamental aspects refer to 'different fields of action and not to frames of mind' (Touraine, 1965, p. 71).

According to Touraine, at the actionalist level the analysis of action should classify some simple elements and their interrelation in order to identify the dynamic principles of transforming one historical system of action into another, or one type of sociopolitical relations into another. Since social action is both *technologically* and *politically* orientated, the concrete technical-political system is constitutive of the historical system of action. There is not necessarily a direct and complete correspondence between a historical system of action and the social system; the distinction between actionalism and functionalism originates here. The same difference exists between the historical system of action and its translation in symbolic forms. These forms, such as for instance myth or Utopian ideologies, can be different from the concrete system of action and cannot be considered as a direct expression of it; hence the distinction between structures of action and structures of the mind, between actionalism and anthropological structuralism.

However, Touraine stresses the interdependence of the three perspectives in order to avoid, on the one hand, an analysis of the historical subject not related to social forms, decision-making levels and concrete sociocultural structures; and also to avoid, on the other hand, the identification of the concrete systems of action with the orientations of action.

As we mentioned above, the concept of the historical subject does not refer to the concrete individual but, like the concept of the social system, must be considered an analytical tool. The analysis of social action in terms of the historical subject is defined by Touraine as 'subjectale' in order to distinguish it from the idealistic 'subjective' approach. The 'subjectale' approach is above all a *sociology of freedom*, that is, an analysis of the creative processes 'through which the forms of social life are constructed and challenged, organized and renewed' (Touraine, 1965, p. 123).

This last aspect, further developed by Touraine in his subsequent books, opens up an evolutive perspective evidently connected with the Marxist tradition. In fact, for Touraine contemporary society seems characterized by the progressive rise of the creative dimension of the historical subject. The change from pre-technological to technological society is interpreted as the evolution from a 'constitutive consciousness' to a 'creative consciousness', the former being characterized by the tendency to project into the natural or social order those values assumed by the latter as a product of its own activity.

Touraine's theoretical project is rightly aimed at pointing out the specific autonomy of action in its relation to the environmental or social conditions, but, despite the complexity of its conceptualization, it is seemingly not entirely successful. Neither the concept of historical subject nor that of labour seem adequate grounds for a theory of social action.

On the one hand, the concept of the historical subject as an analytical tool results in fact from the *ex-post* interpretation of historical processes made by the historian or the social scientist. What is lost in this concept is the pre-reflexive character of action as a real dimension prior to any interpretation. The contradictory and unpredictable character of action risks undervaluation if action is related to a general historical perspective from the standpoint of the social observer. On the other hand, the attempt to use the concept of labour in a wide sense, including both the technological–economical and the cultural–political dimensions, ends up by depriving it of any specific meaning.

The notion of labour as a dialectic relation constitutive of meaning belongs to a well-defined cultural tradition: the question is whether labour has to be considered in itself an autonomous *source* of values or has to be understood as a *product* of historical and social experience, in turn grounded on relatively independent values which give it the character of a fundamental category, as in the case of industrial society.

There is no doubt that labour is a constitutive dimension of praxis and meaning but, just as for every other dimension specific to social situations, it cannot be considered *the* principal factor. Each single dimension is interdependent with the others in a circular relation, out of which a single type of activity can be selected only arbitrarily and analytically as a privileged standpoint.

The technological–economical development is the result of a certain fundamental attitude towards reality and life, which originated in a complex cultural experience connected to a system of social relations. This experience cannot be entirely related to the specific category of labour, even if the latter can be considered an important factor of social change.

It is well known that the identification of action with labour is a constant feature of Western cultural tradition which has been criticized, as already mentioned, by Hannah Arendt (1958), who builds her concept of action precisely on the Aristotelian difference between *praxis* and *poiesis*.

Touraine does not avoid the dilemma common to anyone trying to select an univocal interpretative principle: either the concept of labour is expanded to the point where it merges with the general sense of action, thus losing any explanatory specificity; or, if the specific meaning of labour as production and adaptation is maintained, it leads to a deterministic or functionalistic perspective (see Bubner, 1976). Overlooking the real problem, Touraine seems to vacillate between these two possibilities.

In his more recent studies (Touraine, 1973, 1984), Touraine no longer appears to insist on the concept of labour, but still stresses the creative dimension of the social actor as an active principle of production of social reality. His theory of action, however, does not seem to have undergone any substantial change.

1.5 ACTION AND THE SUBJECT–STRUCTURE RELATION

In this section we shall briefly examine two important theoretical approaches, the first by Pierre Bourdieu and the second by Anthony Giddens, which are both orientated to the deletion of the subjectivism-vs.-structuralism dichotomy. It is well known that Lévi-Strauss's structuralism was deeply influenced by Saussure's theory, which gives priority to the objective system of *langue* over the subjective dimension of *parole*. The different attempts by Foucault, Althusser and Lacan must be considered in this same perspective; they try to eliminate the subjective dimension from the analysis of social or psychological phenomena.

When the individual is reduced to a mere *support* of the structures which are the basis of social reality, as well as the support of the unconscious structures which are the basis of cognitive activities and symbolic representations, action can then no longer be analysed as an autonomous dimension. In the structuralist approach, action is perceived only as a codified *praxis* or as a set of *rules* determining social behaviour: the symbolic-normative determined dimension of action is thus stressed to the detriment of the undetermined dimension of action as an expression of life experience. In this context Austin's (1962) and Searle's (1969) speech act theory becomes a reference for identifying action with language. As will become clearer later, even if it is true that language can be analysed as action, the latter is by no means reducible to language or meaning.

Criticizing both structuralism and subjectivism, Pierre Bourdieu has rightly stressed the methodological fallacy of attributing to the concrete actions of individuals and collectivities the same rational patterns used by the social scientist. Even if no one denies the usefulness of these patterns for the interpretation of social action, they can by no means be considered as principles orientating concrete social activities (see Bourdieu, 1980, p. 25). In Lévi-Strauss's theory, for instance, the structures discovered by the scientist are also conceived of as rules (mainly unconsciously) orientating social behaviour.

Concrete action, according to Bourdieu, follows its own 'logic' which is different from the theoretical logic of the social observer: to recognize that primacy of rationality and structure are principles of intelligibility is not the same as to consider those principles as actually determining action. The social actors, in the course of their actions, do not ask themselves the same questions as the social scientist when he is observing their activities (see Bourdieu, 1980, pp. 53ff.).

To consider that structures are an autonomous reality determining individual behaviour is, for Bourdieu, an 'objectivistic illusion' similar to that which considers *langue* as independent of the speakers. This latter form of illusion is due to the primacy attributed to the inner logic of language over the social conditions of the concrete use of language.

The conflation of theoretical and actional levels apparently solves the opposition between rationally orientated action and structural determinism: 'by introducing rationality, through the notion of unconscious, into the mechanism itself, what was a *Deus ex machina* becomes a *Deus in machina*' (Bourdieu, 1980, p. 69). In this way actions can be considered as 'merely epiphenomenical expressions of the capacity of the structure to develop according to its own laws' (Bourdieu, 1980, p. 70).

For Bourdieu, structuralism ignores the double dimension of the relation between structure and social actors: the structure not only gives orientations to action but is also a *product* of action. Although conditioned by structure, the latter is also permanently transforming it. Structuralism considers only the *structuring* and not also the *structured* character of structure.

The error opposed to that of structuralism is that of *subjectivism* or of voluntaristic decisionism. In a dialectic perspective where the 'mineral opacity of things' is opposed to the 'pure transparency of the subject' (Bourdieu, 1980, p. 73), this approach tends to consider the individual only as a creator of meaning. If objectivism extends the scientific pattern to the point of attributing it to the object of knowledge itself, subjectivism 'generalizes the experience that the subject of the scientific discourse has of himself as a subject' (Bourdieu, 1980, p. 77).

Giving a somewhat reductive interpretation of Sartre's *Critique of Dialectical Reason* and *Methodological Questions*, Bourdieu refers to the Sartrian opposition between the historical action of the subjects and the 'inert' dimension of structures as an example of subjectivism. Praxis, according to Bourdieu, is not a purely mechanical reaction, determined by previous conditions and dependent on pre-established systems of norms and patterns of behaviour, but is also the result of the social actor's free will and conscious intentions (Bourdieu, 1972, p. 178).

Concrete action is at the same time *determined* by conditions and relatively *autonomous*: next to merely mechanical reactions or purely rational actions there are always actions

> which are reasonable without being the result of a rational project; which are oriented by a sort of intrinsic objective teleology, without being consciously organized towards an explicit aim; which are intelligible and coherent without being the result of intentional coherence or free decision; which are adapted to the future, without being the product of a project or a plan. (Bourdieu, 1980, p. 86)

To explain this kind of action, Bourdieu refers to the Aristotelian-Thomistic term *habitus*, namely, those systems of lasting *dispositions* which result from the concrete experience of social life. These dispositions are at the same time *structured* structures, since they are the product of the historical action of individuals and their interrelations, and *structuring* structures, since they generate and organize action as well as individual and collective representations, and thus determine the concrete social situation and the actual possibilities of thought and action.

Bourdieu has undoubtedly contributed by pointing out the limitations of both structuralism and subjectivism, but the concept of *habitus* appears somewhat inadequate to found a theory of the genesis of structures in their relation to social action, and to interpret the dynamics of the subject−structure relation. The concept of *habitus* does not seem to add much to the Parsonian concept of the interiorization of values and norms. In fact, Bourdieu himself defines *habitus* as an inner law implanted in the actor by early upbringing, and as a phenomenon of meaning *reproduction* (see Bourdieu, 1972, p. 180; Bourdieu and Passeron, 1970). Bourdieu tends to historicize those structures that structuralism considered instead to be general dimensions of the collective unconscious; but, in the final analysis, Bourdieu also attributes a primacy to the cultural and normative dimension, thus once again reducing action to meaning.

In order to maintain a character of action irreducible to the normative-symbolic dimension, it is necessary, as will later become clear, to understand the relation between action and structure in terms of the double capacity of subjective consciousness of *identification* with and *distantiation* from the determined forms of symbolic mediation. The whole dimension of action can be recognized only by stressing the *ambivalence* of the attitude of the actor towards those structures, which, although guaranteeing social predictability and intersubjective order, are at the same time limiting his possibilities. In this perspective the negative consequences of determinacy, reached through absolutization, of the normative-symbolic mediation forms become apparent.

In the absence of a theory of the subject in his relation to others and the world, Bourdieu has no adequate means for explaining the genesis of *habitus* and of the dialectic relation between the passive dimension of reproduction and the active creative dimension of change and innovation.

A similar critique can be also applied to Anthony Giddens's theory of social action. Like Bourdieu, Giddens rightly criticizes both subjectivistic and objectivistic univocal approaches, and tries to take into account the *active* as well as the *structural* or *routinized* dimension of action. Giddens defines action as 'a continuous flow of conduct' involving 'a stream of actual or contemplated causal interventions of corporeal beings in the ongoing process of events-in-the-world' (Giddens, 1979, p. 55). Even if he shares the critiques of Marx, Nietzsche and Freud of the concept of consciousness as a unit 'transparent to itself', Giddens does not accept the structuralist tendency to consider the individual only as a product of interrelated meaningful structures. According to Giddens, to conceive of the subject and consciousness as processes rather than substances does not amount to considering them as 'merely epiphenomena of hidden structures. The de-centering of the subject is quite as noxious as the philosophies of consciousness which are attacked if it merely substitutes a structural determination for subjectivity.' Sociological theory should foster 'a recovery of the subject without lapsing into subjectivism' (Giddens, 1979, pp. 40, 44).

Giddens refers to 'the reflexive monitoring of action', that is, its capacity for self-referential regulation. But he also recognizes that a large part of action is based on 'tacit knowledge' or on 'stocks of knowledge', which underlie the processes of production and reproduction of unintentional behaviour. In this perspective action cannot be referred only to the intentionality of social actors, nor to what actors say about the conditions of their actions. Next to intended goals, motivations and reflexive control, there are also the unknown conditions, forms of rationalization, unwanted consequences and codified norms (see Giddens, 1984, pp. 4ff.).

Action and structure are, according to Giddens, mutually dependent within a dialectic process where the dimensions of *time* and *space* are particularly important. Agency and structure are not separate phenomena, they do not represent a dualism, but they should be conceived of as a *duality*: structure is, at the same time, determined by and determining action, and the latter is both a *product* and a *transformative capacity*. In this context Giddens defines structures as rules and resources, or sets of transformative relations which are organized as properties of the social system. The latter is conceived of as a set of relations reproduced among actors or organized collectivities, while *structuration* refers to the set of conditions which regulates the continuity and change of structures, or the reproduction of the social systems (see Giddens, 1984, p. 25).

Giddens, like Bourdieu, rightly considers subject and action as independent variables in relation to objectivated structures, but he does not explain why reference to the subject is still sound even after the critique of subjectivism has been agreed upon. Recognition of the independent impact of subject and structure is insufficient to ground a theory of action; one must also explain how action produces structures and why the first entertains an ambivalent relation with the second. In the absence of such a theoretical development the relation action–structure is mainly interpreted, as in Parsons, in terms of the influence of structure on action through the interiorization of rules and codified practices. Action thus tends to be assimilated to meaning and to the cultural forms which constitute social practices and their reproduction: the autonomous dimension of action, although asserted, is not adequately represented.

1.6 ACTION AND COMMUNICATION

In relation to the theoretical experience of George Mead's symbolic interactionism and of Alfred Schütz's phenomenological sociology, a whole set of different theoretical contributions (Berger and Luckmann's theory of the construction of social reality; Garfinkel's and Cicourel's ethnomethodology; Erving Goffman's interactionist analyses; sociolinguistic theories and so on) have considered action in terms of *sense*, more or less relinquishing the *intentionality* dimension.

All these different approaches stress the impact of *common sense* on social action, that is, the taken-for-granted meanings, social representations and rules which orientate social behaviour in everyday life. In this perspective social action is analysed mainly in terms of the *procedures* and *routines* grounded on the current typifications which support the construction of social reality: action is thus considered as product of an anonymous *interactive order*, within which the creative dimension of the actors tends to disappear.

We shall see later (see Chapter Two, section 2.2, n.2) the difficulties which are met by approaches which stress the primacy of rules; but here, within the context of the aforementioned general orientation of contemporary sociology, I shall consider Jürgen Habermas's theory of communicative action as an attempt to develop a theory of action without any reference to the paradigm of the philosophy of consciousness, and at the same time to establish a non-relativistic ground for rationality.

The fundamental presuppositions of Habermas's theory of action are seemingly two. The first is mainly based on an historical evaluation of the crisis of modernity, through a critical confrontation with the different interpretations given by Marx, Weber, Lukács and Adorno; the second refers to the problem of subjectivity and takes into account the different perspectives of functionalism, structuralism, linguistics and symbolic interactionism.

With regard to the first presupposition, Habermas seems to start from the consideration that in our time Weber's pessimistic predictions have been proved partially untrue: if, on the one hand, the technological development and organizational complexity of our societies have created life conditions which escape more and more from our control, on the other hand, the 'iron cage' has not eliminated, neither at the cultural nor at the social level, a series of *resistances* and *oppositional potentials* against the domineering impact of instrumental rationality (see Habermas, 1981, 1984, 1987).

According to Habermas, the vitality of contemporary social movements and the increasing role of private values prove that Weber's interpretation of modernity was too reductive. The life-world (*Lebenswelt*), where substantial intersubjective communications and processes orientated to mutual understanding take place and where the collective fundamental beliefs spontaneously emerge, shows for Habermas a number of potentialities which are different from those of merely instrumental or purposive rationality. These potentialities have developed thanks to the characteristic process of the modern world, namely the general differentiation of specific meaning and values spheres (law, ethics, religion, politics, science and so on). The differentiation process has allowed a wider collective experience and has opened up new possibilities for different forms of rationality besides the instrumental (that is, ethical, aesthetical and so on), and above all it has favoured the increase of a *communicative* or dialogical rationality, not orientated to efficiency and egotistical goals but to solidarity and co-operation.

If the communicative potentialities of the life-world have been so far obstructed, this, according to Habermas, is due to the predominance of the *social system*, namely, the formal organizational structures of society which result from the logic of market and industrial production, as well as from the political-administrative functions of control. The overall process of rationalization which invested our social reality has split it into the two separate spheres of life-world and social system, and has given undue predominance to the latter. The intrusiveness of the social system into the life-world is interpreted by Habermas in terms of the *internal colonization* of the life-world by the social system. Certain pathological forms of the contemporary life-world (anomie, violence, loss of identity and the rest) are due to the dependence of the latter on the system's imperatives: the communicative forms specific to the life-world are thus replaced by the instrumental-functional forms of the social system (see Habermas, 1987, pp. 196, 356).

The analysis of the progressive *uncoupling of system and life-world* is at the basis of the Habermasian theory of social evolution. Distancing himself from Max Weber, as well as from Lukács's theory of reification and from Horkheimer and Adorno's *Dialectic of Enlightenment*, Habermas wants to provide a positive perspective of our future based on a more balanced relationship between the rationale of economic and technological organization and that of a communicative action orientated to mutual understanding and co-operation. Habermas believes that he has thus also solved the problem of the relation between action and system, which, as mentioned above, had not been adequately formulated by Talcott Parsons.

Habermas's evolutive optimism leads him to establish an analogy between the process of rationalization and differentiation which characterizes the historical evolution of Western society, and the psychological and cognitive development of the individual, as described by Piaget. He interprets historical evolution along the lines of the three levels of moral consciousness (pre-conventional, conventional and post-conventional) suggested by Kohlberg (Habermas, 1984, p. 174).

The tendential internal colonization of the life-world by the social system is no longer considered, as in Adorno, as a fatality specific to the instrumental rationality of the Enlightenment, but as an historically contingent distortion that can be rectified by the potentialities developed through the progressive differentiation of the objective and social worlds from the subjective world of experience: culture and society, individual personality and society, culture and individual personality become in this context increasingly distinct dimensions.

Referring to Durkheim and to Mead, Habermas reformulates the possibility of an actual increase of substantial rationality in the following terms:

> The further the structural components of the lifeworld and the processes that contribute to maintaining them get differentiated, the more interaction contexts come under conditions of rationally motivated mutual understanding, that is of consensus formation that rests *in the end* on the authority of the better argument. (Habermas, 1987, p. 145)

The idea of a 'particularly transparent' life-world is thus no longer used only as a critical reference, but is also perceived as a possible concrete result of sociocultural evolution. Habermas seems here to conflate two levels which he had formerly kept separate: the theory of society and the ideal model of rationality. The reference to a rationality different from the instrumental one was, in fact, since the beginning a characteristic feature of Habermas's approach (see Habermas, 1968), but only in the present theoretical development is communicative rationality also perceived as a concrete product of historical evolution. Hence, there is a shift from the previous critical approach, connected with the tradition of Weber and Adorno, to the present evolutive approach which, despite its sophistication, seems more in line with the Utopian Marxist tradition (see Honneth, 1982; Arnason, 1980).

In order to understand the significance of this theoretical change it is necessary to consider the second aforementioned presupposition, which is at the basis of the predominance acquired by the communicative structures in the Habermasian approach. I am referring to the explicit denial of the 'consciousness paradigm' in favour of the structural paradigm of *communicative rationality*, which Habermas defines as 'the medium of symbolic reproduction of the lifeworld'. Criticizing the consciousness dimension specific to Adorno's aesthetics, Habermas maintains that the rational core of mimetic achievements

> can be laid open only if we give up the paradigm of the philosophy of consciousness – namely, a subject that represents objects and toils with them – in favor of the paradigm of linguistic philosophy – namely, intersubjective understanding or communication – which puts the cognitive-instrumental aspect of reason in its proper place as part of a more encompassing *communicative rationality*. (Habermas, 1984, p. 390)

Intersubjective relations and relations to the natural world are thus no longer analysed according to the philosophy of consciousness with which Husserl interpreted the life-world. They are now seen instead as 'interconnections of meaning holding between a given communicative utterance, the immediate context and its connotative horizon of meaning', these interconnections being nothing else than 'grammatically regulated relations' (Habermas, 1987, p. 124).

Taking as the essential reference the fundamental structures of communication, Habermas analyses the ways in which social actors establish their relations with 'something which is there in the world' through their symbolic expressions. This 'something' can be *objective* (the natural world), *social* (the social institutions) and *subjective* (the inner world). In accordance with these different modalities, three general *validity claims* are distinguished: namely, the proposition content is *true* (*wahr*), the performative component is *correct* (*richtig*) and the intentions are being expressed *sincerely* (*wahrhaftig*). These validity claims form the rational basis underlying every act of communication, and constitute the background consensus of normally functioning language games. On this basis it is possible to establish a general criterion for the ideal conditions of a discourse coherent with the presuppositional validity claims and free from any distortion. I shall not analyse in detail this fundamental issue of Habermas's theory; I shall only try to show some of its general consequences for the theory of action.

Distancing himself from the *phenomenological* approach in favour of the *communicative*, Habermas, under the influence of Apel's (1973) theory of the ideal situation of unlimited communication, believes that the essential rules of communication provide a positive basis for a form of rationality which avoids the risks of falling, on the one hand, into the transcendental subjectivism common to metaphysics and Husserlian phenomenology, as well as, on the other hand, into the objectivism characteristic of a certain historicism. This basis appears in fact to be open to empirical falsification and does not have an absolute character, although it is universal and binding: it should allow one to avoid both the relativism of Nietzschean nihilism and the subjectivism of the different forms of existentialism. Being grounded on a new positive form of rationality, critical theory thus seems to be no longer bound to the negative approach of Adorno's dialectics, and to be capable of providing a constructive perspective on social emancipation.

But the price that Habermas has to pay for this achievement appears to be very high. In the final analysis, the denial of the consciousness dimension hinders any acknowledgement of the *limits* of symbolic order and actually establishes an identity between action and meaning, action and language. The possibility of detecting the inner contradictions of practical experience and social dynamics is thus highly compromised.

I am not trying to revive here, in opposition to Habermas, the traditional philosophy of consciousness. As mentioned above (see Chapter One, section 1.1), the contemporary critique of this philosophy has evidenced the illusory nature of the pure transparency of self-consciousness and has demonstrated that our consciousness cannot be conceived of as the centre of invariably free and rational decisions. Social sciences have definitely stressed the formative relevance of cultural patterns, language, values and normative orders of society for the constitution of self.

But if subjective consciousness cannot in itself be considered as the origin of meaning and the foundation of reality, it is nevertheless also evident that human experience cannot be explained without referring to the negative capacity of the ego to differentiate itself from the many forms of objectivation, both external (representations of the world, norms and so on) and internal, that serve to establish the identity of the individual: 'that consciousness which, distancing itself from everything that exists, can also distance itself from its own personality' (Valéry, 1957, p. 420).

What I call the negative dimension of consciousness is in fact implicit in any discourse about subjectivity, and even Habermas cannot avoid it when he refers to speaking actors, capable of reflexivity and action. Language, the possibility of mutual understanding through forms of symbolic mediation, the reciprocity and solidarity which emerge in social action, make sense only with reference to individuals who, precisely because they are self-conscious, are never *immediately* identified with their phenomenal reality, but instead make constant use of symbolic *mediation* forms from which they keep a certain distance. Without that distance there would not, in fact, be *symbolic* or *normative* communication, but only a reactive exchange of signs and stimuli, as in the animal world.

Without reference to the negative dimension of consciousness, it is no longer possible to distinguish between life experience (*Erlebnis*) and symbolic forms, and thus the reductive role of the latter is never shown. Despite having asserted elsewhere that the identity of the ego is strengthened by assuming a critical attitude towards institutionalized roles, symbolic forms and social expectations (see Habermas, 1976), Habermas tends to fall into a sort of absolutization of the communicative dimension. This leads him to underestimate the contradictions and ambivalence that characterize our relationship to the forms of symbolic mediation, giving way to a new form of the ideal of a transparent society common in Marxian tradition.

In his denial of the paradigm of consciousness, Habermas is after all seemingly influenced by the same ideal of general scientific objectivity which has led Lévi-Strauss to apply the patterns of Saussurian linguistics to kinship relations and myth, and Lacan to compare the unconscious to language (see Roustang, 1986).

The structural analysis is fully adequate when applied to determined forms, such as objects or relations among objects: it is perfectly reasonable to analyse the structure of a tree, a car, a painting, a linguistic code or a text, and even, as we shall see later, of the objectified 'traces' of action. Lévi-Strauss has in fact achieved his best results in the application of the structuralist pattern to the rules of matrimonial exchange. But the same approach becomes inadequate when, next to the naturally or symbolically determined forms, we have to deal with the indeterminate dimensions of actual action, these dimensions being strictly connected to the aforementioned capacity of distantiation from the objectified forms typical of the unconditional character of subjective action.

Since every form of determinacy (the identity of the individual included) is historically and socially conditioned, the freedom of action can only be conceived in terms of a *shifting*, through successive negations and reconstructions, from one form to another of determinacy. Provided that the primacy of the negative dimension of consciousness — which shows that, in the last analysis, the ego is not reducible to identity — is duly recognized, the reference to consciousness does not necessarily involve either the transcendental dimension of subjectivity — for even the Kantian categories can be interpreted as rules of the symbolic determinacy — or the nihilistic aspects of Adorno's dialectic, for the negation of objectified forms is at the origin of any creative pragmatic project (see Crespi, 1986).

In denying the phenomenological approach to consciousness, Habermas has no other choice than to develop a sort of structuralist analysis of the communicative forms. The tendency to identify the entire social reality to the cognitive and communicative structures becomes evident in the way in which the life-world is defined by Habermas. Even though he recognizes that the life-world has an organic basis and a pre-reflexive character, he never allows for a phenomenology of life experience, assuming that the analysis of language that shows the structures of the life-world is 'more promising' than the phenomenological attempts to reconstruct life dynamics. In this context Habermas does not avoid that sort of 'idealism' of communication that he has himself attributed to hermeneutics.

After having criticized Schütz and Luckmann for being bound to the paradigm of the philosophy of consciousness and having denounced the 'culturalistic reduction' of the life-world, Habermas actually defines in purely cultural or procedural terms the essential functions of communicative action. These functions are thus identified as: *mutual understanding*, namely, tradition and renewal of cultural knowledge; *co-ordinating action*, namely, social integration and solidarity; and *socialization*, namely the building up of social identities. *Culture*, *society* and *persons* correspond to these functions 'as structural components of the life-world'. But here again, culture is defined as a 'stock of knowledge', society as 'legitimate order' and personality as 'the competences' that make a subject capable of speaking and acting (Habermas, 1987, pp. 137–8).

The fact that everything is defined in cultural or normative terms explains why Habermas tends to stress the *background* character of the life-world. This is considered as a set of conditions which, although being accessible to knowledge in principle, do not in fact pertain to the thematically relevant aspects of the situation. The life-world is 'the intuitively present, in this sense familiar and transparent and at the same time vast and incalculable, web of presuppositions that are to be satisfied if an actual utterance is to be all meaningful' (Habermas, 1987, p. 131).

It is certainly true that the forms of symbolic-normative mediation which regulate social relations in everyday life function precisely because, being taken for granted, they do not have to be analysed again each time. But it is nevertheless also true that those rules and those representations are constantly kept in tension against the continuous rise of unpredictable events and against the feeling of bewilderment and uneasiness (*Unheimische*) which is the fundamental tonality of our existential situation as such.

It is precisely in order to cope with these indeterminate dimensions that every society develops a number of mechanisms of latent control based on taken-for-granted representations and rules. Habermas himself does recognize that individuals in the life-world 'certainly live with the *awareness of the risk* that some unforeseeable event may happen'. But in Habermas's theory there is no way to explain that awareness which is connected to the specific capacity of consciousness to distance itself from any determined form: in fact, Habermas hastens to add that awareness 'cannot shatter the naïve trust in the life-world' (Habermas, 1987, p. 132). Now the question is not the persistence of naïve trust, for trust is an essential condition for survival and psychological welfare; the question is how that awareness can be theoretically grounded.

We can, in fact, understand this awareness only by relating it to the specific negative capacity of consciousness to perceive the limitations of the forms of symbolic determinacy (representations, norms, codified procedures and so on) which guarantee predictability. Even when this capacity is only potential, it deeply characterizes our relation with the symbolic forms, pervading our everyday life world: a world where there are not only interpersonal communications orientated to consensus, but also continuous misunderstandings, conflicts, fears and anxieties.

With no means of conceptualizing the reductive character of the symbolic forms and our ambivalent relation to them, Habermas's theory, despite the opposition between life-world and social system, surprisingly lacks dramatic aspects. Having considered the presuppositions of Habermas's theory and some of its fundamental limitations, I shall try to summarize briefly my critical observations about it:

(a) The idealization of the communicative dimension, and the predominant role attributed to it, tends to conceal in Habermas's theory the reductive character of the forms of symbolic mediation through which any communication develops. By *reductive* I mean that the complexity of action, as I have already pointed out, can never be entirely expressed by determinate forms of language and norms. Determination is always obtained through *absolutization*: truth, certainty, predictability result from the elimination of the indeterminacy proper to complexity. The symbolic-normative forms are thus contradictory in themselves, being at the same time *reductive* and *absolutized*. This explains our ambivalent relation to them: the need of determinacy to establish personal identity and social order leads the social actors to identify themselves with the determinate forms, but the reductive character of the latter is often perceived as a limitation obstructing the free expression of experience and action. Hence the negative attitude towards the objectified forms and the distantiation from them, the possibility of change and innovation connected with the risk of insecurity. Beside the functional *observance of rules* we can thus consider the functional *non-observance of rules*: no social organization can function without the observance of norms, nor at the same time without infringement of these same norms (see Chapter Four, section 4.1).

The dismissal of the paradigm of consciousness prevents an adequate analysis of these contradictions and ambivalences and tends to ignore the fact that determinacy can be equally as destructive of society as indeterminacy. When this aspect is taken into account, then communication appears rather as a sort of compromise reached through negotiation among different interpreters than, as in Habermas, as the expression of a transparent consensus of rational values. Although Habermas would reply to this that he is not considering the communicative situation as an empirical reality but as an ideal criterion of reference, it nevertheless seems that even an 'ideal' model should at least correspond to the essential character of the considered process. The symbolic order, being always a determined selection from numerous possibilities, cannot be equally gratifying to every member of society. The variety of individual situations, linked to class and ethnic differences as well as to variations in life experiences, results in different degrees of agreement with the prevailing symbolic-normative forms of society. Consequently it appears, as we shall see later (Chapter Four, section 4.4), that the symbolic order itself becomes a source of inequality and conflict.

The ideal communicative situation is thus impossible not only for empirical reasons due to complexity but also because in itself it contradicts the reductive character of symbolic mediation.

(b) The dismissal of the paradigm of consciousness in concealing the difference between action and communication, prevents the recognition that action, which is prior to any comprehension or sense (see Chapter Three), has an ambivalent relation with the symbolic-normative forms which has to be dealt with by discretional *judgement*, *phronesis* and *power* (see Chapter Four).

These dimensions cannot adequately be interpreted within Habermas's procedural world, which, in its evolutionary perspective, appears to be intrinsically orientated towards an ideal consensual solution of the social problem, instead of towards the acknowledgement of the irreconcilable character of the social situation as such.

(c) The pretence of founding an absolute criterion of rationality on validity claims implicit in any communication appears objectionable. To my knowledge, validity claims are no more than functional rules of discourse, that is, one could consider them merely as rules necessary to sustain the *fiction* of communication, as conditions for the production of determinate patterns in order to establish social predictability and co-ordination. Mutual communication is possible even when, as is often the case, the actors interact only *as if* they were saying the truth, *as if* they were observing the social rules and *as if* they were sincere. To presume that communicative validity claims are the ideal ground of ethics and justice can thus be only the result of a choice to do so. This certainly deserves respect but the fact that some rules are absolutely required entails only their instrumental necessity.

(d) The disjunction between life-world and social system which is at the basis of Habermas's interpretation of modernity, appears only as the pale image of the deeper tension existing between life experience and symbolic order. In fact, life-world and social system have the same roots in Habermas's theory: on the one hand, the characteristic presuppositions of language which found *communicative* rationality are also at the basis of *instrumental* or purposive rationality; on the other hand, the hypertrophic dimensions of the social system in modern society are the consequence of the same evolutive process involving the life-world. The possibility of establishing a new balance between life-world and social system is based precisely on the fact that both life-world and social system are conceived by Habermas as dimensions internal to the symbolic-normative order.

At this point, despite Habermas's complex analysis of the evolution of the modern world, it is difficult to understand why the same process 'of the successive releases of the potential for rationality in communicative action' (Habermas, 1987, p. 155) has ended up in producing a pathological increase in the complexity of the system, giving way to the systemic imperatives which have exploited the life-world. This process could well be interpreted in terms of the tendency to absolutization typical of the determined and reductive forms of symbolic mediation: in this case, what seems to have been absolutized is the univocal dimension of instrumental rationality. But, as I have already said, there are no elements in Habermas's theory for this type of interpretation.

In Habermas's perspective the opposition between life-world and social system seems to be the result of ideological choice rather than empirical analysis. With reference to concrete social relations, it is in fact difficult to isolate instrumental strategies, orientated to interests and success, from communicative actions, orientated to mutual understanding and solidarity. In concrete social processes these different components are always intertwined, so that, for instance, the economic and administrative levels are constantly interfered with by dimensions which Habermas would consider as specific to the life-world. Many empirical studies show, on the one hand, how much formal organizations are deeply influenced by informal relations based on friendship, kinship links, patronage and so on; and, on the other hand, how much the systemic dimensions of politics, economic interests and social services are influencing the private life of the individual, orientating his psychology and conditioning his identity and the choices of his everyday life, as well as his interpersonal relations.

There is no reason to consider these interrelations as pathological: social solidarity develops through economic relations, just as purposive actions could not develop without a certain degree of co-operation. The drives underlying the strategic actions of the political and economic world have their roots in the life-world, whereas the latter is never merely the result of the *colonization* process by the social system.

What, in the last analysis, deeply divides social reality is not the disjunction between life-world and social system, but the fact that life experience and action are not reducible to the symbolic-normative order. The distortions common to social reality are mainly due to the difficulty of dealing with the specific contradictions of the reification processes which are produced by absolutization of the forms of symbolic mediation, or else with contradictions which result from an excessive degree of indeterminacy produced by uncontrolled actions. A partial solution to this problem has to be sought, as we shall see later (Chapter Four), through an increase of the individual and collective capacity to deal with the contradictions which emerge from the relation between the determinacy of normative-communicative order and the indeterminacy of action.

(e) Surprisingly, Habermas's recent theoretical positions appear to be nearer to Luhmann's approach than to the critical tradition of the Frankfurt School (see Donati, 1987). Common to both Habermas and Luhmann is the rejection of the paradigm of consciousness, while the evolutive conception stressing the differentiation of spheres of values and the relevance given to the phenomenon of communication are similar in both. If the opposition between life-world and social system is alien to Luhmann's theory, in Habermas, as I have tried to show, rather than being rooted in essential differences, it appears to be the result of an ideological choice.

Habermas's goal of unifying action and system theories in one synthetic approach has not been achieved, precisely because his concept of action is too weak. In failing to show the difference between action and symbolic communication, the Habermasian approach, even if it avoids the causal explanation of action as a result of the social system, tends to overlook the specific dimension of action and thus becomes another version of the systemic theory.

1.7 WHERE TO FIND ACTION

Our brief critical appraisal of the most important theoretical approaches to social action in contemporary sociology has shown, on the one hand, that there is a common orientation towards the critique of the merely objectivistic approaches, which stresses the creative dimension of action; and on the other hand, that there is a common tendency to overevaluate the determined symbolic-normative dimension of action, by removing the dimensions more directly connected to life experience and to the undetermined character of action.

When society is analysed mainly in terms of values and patterns of behaviour, the impact of cultural elements is fatally overestimated to the detriment of the interpretation of actual social relations which, although they are largely the product of the *observance* of norms and codified social models, can also be regarded as the result of a constant *infringement* of these norms and models.

I believe that the specific character of sociological analysis can be maintained only by recognizing and interpreting the ambivalent character of the relation between action and symbolic order. There is here, of course, a challenge to sociological knowledge, for life experience as such necessarily escapes empirical observation. The latter has in fact to be developed through a partial selection of aspects out of a stream of complex relations.

Referring somewhat to Heisenberg's principle of indeterminacy, one could say that the more we are orientated to scientific knowledge, the less we can perceive life experience, while the more we want to grasp life experience, the less 'objective' will be our results. This tension between subjectivism and scientific rigorism was clearly analysed by Husserl in *The Crisis of European Sciences*.

It seems that the specific contribution of sociology must take place at the intermediate point between the extremes of absolute abstraction and total concreteness, showing, through a constant oscillation between these two poles, some aspects of reality which otherwise would be ignored. In this perspective Max Weber's cognitive attitude appears much more adequate than the positivistic, notwithstanding his tendency to identify action with intentional meaning. Weber's *ideal types* are, in fact, conceived as abstract and limited tools constantly referring to a reality whose complexity cannot be exhausted.

On the basis of our previous critical analysis, we can now claim, first, that a more adequate understanding of action should show how the cultural dimension is generated by action before orientating it; secondly, that there is an unmeasurable dimension of action limiting our capacity for predictability and understanding, this dimension being an essential reference in order not to lose sight of the specific character of the social situation.

In the following pages I shall try to show that an adequate theory of social action should free itself from every totalitarian pretence characteristic of the teleological paradigm of our cultural tradition. As stressed by the phenomenological analysis both of the first and the second Heidegger, the primacy attributed within that tradition to the cognitive dimension and to purposive rationality has removed the ontological dimension: when the latter is duly recognized it then appears that action cannot be interpreted only through causal factors or normative principles, but emerges as a multidimensional reality 'having no reason' and as previous to any conscious determination of intentionality and values (see Schürmann, 1982).

When perceived against the background of the ontological dimension, the unmeasurable character of action explains, on the one hand, the capacity of the social actor to transcend up to a certain degree the symbolic-normative orders and contrast 'reality' with a radically cynical attitude (Diogenes), disrespectful of authority and 'truth' (see Sloterdijk, 1983).

On the other hand, going from the ontological to the historical level, the pre-predicative character of action can be interpreted, as we shall better expound later, in terms of social actors' belonging to the sociocultural context which determines the horizon of their concrete possibilities. In this way the risk of falling into some form of methodological individualism or idealism can be avoided.

The connection between the unobjectivable character of life experience and action shows that action is a *borderline concept* for sociological theory, the reference to which is, however, essential for a non-reductive empirical analysis of social reality. This analysis can, in fact, be developed only by taking into account the particular position of the individual in his relation with the practical determinations of action and the forms of symbolic-normative mediation.

The objection could be raised at this point that the general categories of action I am referring to have in fact 'metaphysical' assumptions. I think it is time to answer this objection by recognizing that *any* theoretical approach starts from some philosophical presupposition and that the decision to reduce action to a merely utilitarian calculus or to a purely symbolic-normative dimension, is by no means less aprioristic.

When, for instance, Max Weber analyses the functions of religion, he refers to general categories such as the problem of happiness and sorrow;

the need to give sense to life and to answer 'to the absurdity of questions and events'; guilt feelings; the problem of inequality between merit and success; the problem of death, and so on (see Weber, 1922). These different interpretative categories, which implicitly refer to an existential or anthropological conception, are not analysed by Weber as such, but rather are used as taken-for-granted presuppositions in order to understand the manifold questions to which the great world religions of the past tried to give an answer.

As we shall see later (Chapter Two, section 2.2), even those sociologists who, as ethnomethodologists, want to stick to a pure 'indexicality', end up by implicitly referring to general psychological or existential categories.

Every time we define something we are absolutizing what we are saying: thus there is no point in trying to avoid in our discourse every aprioristic or metaphysical element. The difference between a scientific and a philosophic discourse lies in the fundamental orientation towards the categories that are used: if the philosopher considers his categories *true*, the social scientist will use them as interpretative tools, whose validity must be proved through their *usefulness* within the specific perspective adopted, in order to understand the complex phenomenon under observation (see Chapter Five).

Adopting general categories does not prevent the sociologist from analysing the concrete historical and cultural forms and the specific meanings of life experience, as well as the particular degree of awareness of them, which vary in time and space: it is precisely these variations that have to be interpreted, by adapting and eventually changing our interpretative tools.

Every society, starting from 'primitive' ones, has dealt with the problem of preventing dangerously deviant behaviours by reinforcing a symbolic-normative order. Similarly, even if there were cultures where the individual dimension or the negative capacity of consciousness did not explicitly emerge, every society must face the problem of elaborating at the practical level some form of reassurance about its identity. These circumstances show that, despite the great differences in the contingent situations, the capacity for distancing from the objectivated forms has been a permanent condition of social life, underlying the precariousness of its order as well as its ambivalences and contradictions. No *history* would, after all, be possible without reference to general categories which permit the establishment of comparisons between different epochs and infer changes in time and space.

On the basis of these first presuppositions, our search for action will be developed through a confrontation with the contemporary experience of phenomenology and hermeneutics: that experience has in fact been grounded on the relationship between life experience and cognitive forms, as well as on the interrelation between action and language.

2

Action as a Borderline Concept

'Saying is not exhausted by what is said.'

E. Lévinas

2.1 THE REDUCTION OF ACTION TO MEANING

Summarizing the conclusions of his critical appraisal of the different theories of action, Rüdiger Bubner writes:

> The concept of action has been defined, without exception, through another concept, which is actually at the centre of the attention. This shifting from one concept to another can be explained by the systematic attitude of the theory of action, which finds its expression within a set of categorical concepts or general frames of reference. The term replacing the concept of action is always that of 'meaning', even if the latter may refer, according to the circumstances, to completely different things. (Bubner, 1976, p. 52)

It is easy to understand why the concept of action tends to be replaced by that of meaning. As I have already said, when knowledge is being orientated towards descriptive and value-free *neutrality*, as the only basis for rationality and science, then the concept of action becomes a nuisance. As Lévi-Strauss has rightly perceived, to obtain an exact science one must *'répudier le vécu'* (Lévi-Strauss, 1955, p. 50). On the one hand, since action, as opposed to the concept of behaviour, has always to be referred to subjectivity, it appears to be fatally opposed to the aforementioned idea of science, for it stresses precisely those dimensions of affective and evaluative *un-neutrality* and unpredictability which undermine the model of natural sciences.

On the other hand, no serious social scientist would today be inclined simply to adopt the deterministic patterns of positivistic tradition: after the experience of German historicism, and particularly of Max Weber, the historical and cultural dimension of social phenomena can no longer be ignored.

A way out from this dilemma seems to be offered by stressing *meaning*, as a set of codified significances and rules specific to a concrete form of society. Subjectivity loses in this case its unpredictable quality and appears as the *product* of the values and patterns of behaviour of the cultural system. In this way the acknowledgement of the historical and cultural dimension is no longer contradictory to the ideal of scientific objectivity. It is in this context that Weber refers to the 'spirit' of the times (*Zeitgeist*) and to the ideal types of action, focusing on the *intentionated meaning* and on the cultural patterns which determine the latter.

An even more reassuring 'solution' is that offered by Lévi-Strauss's structuralism: linguistic structuralism defies the philosophy of subjectivity, and identifies meaning with language, as an autonomous system articulated by its own inner differences (see Hjemslev, 1943; Ricoeur, 1969).

In the latter perspective, it is even no longer necessary to take into account the historical contents of the objectified meaning, but it is sufficient to refer to the general laws regulating the production of concrete cultural forms, thus removing any aspect connected to subjective experience: social actors merely become the support of constant structures which can be identified through the seeming disorder of specific cultural forms.

In Habermas too, as we have already seen, the rejection of the paradigm of consciousness leads to conceiving the life-world as a communicative structure essentially derived from the rules of language. Similarly, the influence of structuralism could be detected in the recent developments of symbolic interactionism, Erving Goffman and ethnomethodology.

While not ignoring the important contributions of these different approaches, one has to admit that in fact they wipe out the specific dimension of action. As I have said before, structuralism can be adequately applied to the objectified forms of both nature and culture, but it is totally inadequate to analyse action, which emerges not only from *determinate* factors but also from the *indeterminate* elements proper to the relatively unconditional character of subjectivity.

Action thus appears to elude the intents of scientific predictability and neutrality. The question now is whether we have to give up the concept of action and fall back on empirical behaviourism, or whether the reference to action is essential to understand social dynamics in a less reductive way than that offered by the analysis of the rules of communication or by statistical surveys. By now I think it will be clear enough that for real *sociological* knowledge the reference to action is essential.

The removal of the specific dimension of action leads to a conception of society as a potentially integrated order (functional system, ideal situation of communication and so on), whereas the recognition that action is not reducible to meaning or language leads to conceiving of society in terms of an irreconcilable situation characterized by the contradiction between the indeterminate dimension of action and the determined forms of symbolic-normative order. The first position is mainly orientated towards increasing rational *normative order* while the second seeks an increase of *power*, that is, the capacity at both individual and collective level of dealing with the unavoidable contradictions of the social condition (see Chapter Four).

The *focus* of sociological analysis, as compared to social psychology or to cultural anthropology, thus appears to be strictly connected with the concept of power, along the lines that will be considered later.

The relative autonomy of action with respect to meaning shows that action cannot be analysed only through motivations or cultural forms. In the following pages I shall try to show, through a critical appraisal of the philosophy of praxis as well as of phenomenology and hermeneutics, how sociological theory can take into account the uncommensurable dimension of action. However, before considering the contributions of these different approaches, I shall further develop the analysis of some general aspects of the relationship between action and normative order.

2.2 OBSERVANCE OF RULES AND RELATION TO RULES

In Wittgenstein's theoretical perspective of the connection between language games and forms of life, the analysis of the phenomenon of 'following a rule' has undoubtedly enriched the Weberian approach to the interpretation of social action. However, the positive results of that analysis must also be evaluated by recognizing some of its limitations and by denouncing some of its illusions. In order to make my argument clear enough, I shall distinguish the epistemological and the empirical aspects of the problem even though, obviously, they are strictly interrelated.

Let us consider first the *epistemological level*. One of the major contributions given by reference to the rules, as normative criteria orientating both social representations and concrete actions, is a better understanding of the difference between social and natural sciences, along the lines developed by Peter Winch (1958). The analytical criteria of natural science only belong to the observer, while in social sciences the criteria reflexively applied by social actors to their own actions appear to be at least as relevant as those applied by the social scientist. In this last perspective, the analysis of the empirical *regularities* of action has to be necessarily connected to the *rules* by which these regularities are being defined by both the social actors and the social scientist who interpret them (see Winch, 1958). Knowledge of the rules is thus based on the awareness of the rules of knowledge shared by the social actors themselves, as well as of those shared by social scientists. The epistemological ethnocentrism of the social scientist is thus overcome and the analysis of action appears in its true character as a hermeneutical exchange among different interpretations, with all the difficulties deriving from the dimensions of tradition, translation and betrayal which characterize it (see Gadamer, 1972).

Besides providing a better understanding of the specific character of sociological knowledge as compared to that of common sense (although opening the problem of the grounding of scientific knowledge differently from that of other forms of construction of social reality – see Chapter Five), the attention given to rules in their connection with meaning has also the advantage of releasing the interpretation of action from reference to aprioristic self-related paradigms independent from the concrete context of social actors' activities. I am referring here to the aforementioned interpretative paradigms based on the biological structure of natural needs or on the psychological structures of utilitarian rationality, and so on. Through the notion of rules, it seems in fact that the analysis of action can be developed by taking into account only the current criteria ruling concrete social situations, in their connection with material conditions.

If it is true that the reference to rules partly achieves this result, releasing sociological interpretation from many 'metaphysical' presuppositions, it is, however, also true that a total identification with the merely empirical context of action appears to be illusory.

Particularly in the first phase of its development, ethnomethodology claimed for itself the status of the only true scientific sociological approach, on the grounds that, following the principle of indexicality, its analyses were developed only by reference to the rules shared by social actors (see Garfinkel, 1967). This claim has met with serious difficulties. The ethnomethodologists themselves, or at least the most aware among them, had to recognize that the interpretative process develops not only from the encounter between the criteria of social actors and social scientists, but also from reference to some general presuppositions common to both. Without this common ground no exchange would be actually possible. The general principles of formal logic and a number of general psychological categories seem to be unavoidable implicit presuppositions of any interpretation of action. Our analyses originate within a system of meta-rules, which in turn cannot be totally analysed: thus a pure indexicality is never entirely achieved.

Aaron Cicourel has shown that any analysis of the circumstances and specific rules which constitute a social event can give way to ever new interpretations of the *same* circumstances and of the *same* rules. Similarly, the criteria orientating the social scientist's analysis can also be endlessly analysed (what are the criteria of analysis of the criteria of analysis of the criteria of analysis? – and so on). This means that every interpretation develops through a relatively arbitrary selection of aspects made by the social scientist. If there can be methods of analysis which are more sophisticated than others, no method is essentially different from the traditional empirical procedures labelled by the ethnomethodologists as 'folk sociology', even though the latter were much less aware of their constructive character and of their limitations.

Both Garfinkel and Cicourel have tried to find a way out of the problem of total indexicality by referring to the *invariant forms* of interpretative procedures, of both social actors and social scientists, or to *basic procedures*, analogous to those of language, Chomsky's generative grammar and cognitive psychology. All these different approaches actually revive, in different ways, the reference to aprioristic rational or psychological paradigms (see Cicourel, 1973; Crespi, 1985, p. 275).

Quoting Gadamer's concept of 'fusion of horizons', Charles Taylor has rightly stressed that the concepts of rules and forms of life lead to a hermeneutic exchange: 'the adequate language in which we can understand another society is not our language of understanding, or theirs, but rather what one could call a language of perspicuous contrast' (Taylor, 1981, p. 205). Referring to Winch (1964) in this same context, Taylor observes that the forms of life of our and other societies can be understood as 'alternative possibilities in relation to some *human constants* at work in both' (Taylor, ibid.).

The analysis which stresses the contextuality of meanings orientating action also appears to be developed through reference to human constants, both existential and cognitive. This shows that the principle of indexicality has bounds and that action cannot be interpreted merely with reference to rules. The question then is how to conceive of the human constants: this problem has to be considered in relation to the aforementioned *empirical level* of the analysis of rules.

The consequences of the reference to human constants, both as invariant forms of interpretative procedures (Cicourel) and as basic elements of experience and action (Winch, Taylor), can be better understood by analysing the concrete relations between action and rules. According to Winch, the concept of meaningful action implies reference to rules as constitutive elements of action as such. Winch, quoting Weber, has rightly emphasized that the meaning of an action takes shape only within a context where that action is intertwined with other actions in a temporal dimension involving the future: meaningful interrelated actions are symbolic, that is, they predetermine future behaviours (see Winch, 1958, p. 67). There is thus an intimate link connecting meaning, social context, rules and time.

The possibility of analytically distinguishing action from rule results from the fact that there are different rules and different ways to observe or infringe a rule. A rule can be identified both through the interpretation of the social scientist and through the self-reflexive awareness of the actors, but when so defined it appears to be a determinate reduction of the complexity of life experience. It is thus only as *complexity* that action can be distinguished from the specific rules which orientate it.

Complexity as such cannot be directly comprehended (action as a 'borderline concept') but, starting from the presupposition that there is no meaningful action without rule, complexity can be considered as the possibility of *shifting* from one rule to another, or as the possibility of *diversified modalities* of reference to a rule. From this standpoint it seems that understanding in abstract the constitutive link between meaningful action and rule is something different from considering the concrete relation established in a specific situation between a determined rule and an action, for the latter is the result not only of the social but also of the subjective elaboration of the set of rules that, within the course of time, has allowed the structuring of that particular action. The merely external observance of a rule as such does not reveal the entire meaning of the actor's experience, which is qualified also by the specific relation that the actor has established with the same rule.

When we take into account the distinction between *personal identity*, namely, the inner, conscious and unconscious, elaboration of his biographical experience made by the actor, and *social identity*, namely, the external self-image given by the individual to others in interactional and communicative processes (see Crespi, 1985, pp. 367ff.), we become aware of the different degrees of integration or conflict between the inner and outer attitudes of the social actor, and we understand how the observance of a rule can have manifold meanings.

The fact that a concrete behaviour can be interpreted using the rules of the social context within which the behaviour takes place, does not yet reveal anything about the actual attitude of the individual towards those same rules. The observance of the same rule can assume a different meaning for each social actor, while observance of different rules can have a similar meaning for the actors themselves. The identification of the social rules is therefore a necessary but insufficient condition for interpreting action and its social effects.

A given ritual behaviour, such as going to church on Sundays, may appear perfectly clear once I know the traditional rules shared by the actors who assume that behaviour, but I will still not know if the observance of that rule is the result of a full correspondence between the actor's inner and outer representations, or if it is the product of a merely formal compliance, the passive acceptance of tradition, opportunism, or even a latent opposition to the same rule, and so on.

The distinction between personal and social identity leads to a typology of relations to rules according to the degree of correspondence or non-correspondence between inner and outer attitudes, the degree of flexibility or rigidity (absolutization or relativization) of the normative system, the explicit or implicit (conscious–unconscious, manifest–latent) character of the rules, and so on (see Crespi, 1985, pp. 463ff.). In the sociological perspective, the problem is not to interpret each specific attitude of the individuals but to show the variety of codified meanings and forms of awareness specific to the social context under consideration. Beyond the manifest rules one must detect the latent interpretative rules which are current in the social situation under analysis, showing its potential conflicts and tensions.

The manifold meanings that can be assumed by the observance of a rule, not to mention the specific meanings of infringement or deviance from the rules, show that there is no identity between action and norm, as the different ways of referring to norms cannot be translated into rules. The complexity of 'following a rule' leads to a theoretical paradigm adequate to consider the ambivalent relation between action and forms of symbolic-normative mediation. As a matter of fact, even empirical analyses of social action which try to eliminate all reference to subjective motivations by sticking to indexicality, cannot entirely avoid referring to some general psychological or existential categories.

Goffman's attempt to reduce the individual to a mere social role cannot be developed to its ultimate consequences. The explanation of the differentiation of the social actors' attitudes towards their roles, as well as of the deviations from or elusions of the role prescriptions, frequently forces Goffman to refer to categories such as self-defence, continuity of identity in the course of time, self-image coherence, and so on. The actor's *need for reassurance* through the determination of his individual and social status, or his opposing need to *keep a distance* from the social roles to avoid being taken for granted as well as to ensure his freedom and power in his relation with others, are all categories based on some implicit general presuppositions about the existential situation as such (see Goffman, 1959, 1961).

Similarly, the ethnomethodological surveys showing the actors' anxiety and stress consequent on the induced shattering of the taken-for-granted rules in everyday life, make sense only by reference to implicit presuppositions deriving from a general conception of the existential situation, such as the anxiety of self-conscious individuals due to unpredictability and lack of certainty, their need of determinacy, and so on. Despite the fact that their theories are mainly based on such implicit presuppositions, neither Goffman nor the ethnomethodologists seem to analyse the specific character of these presuppositions.

Our considerations both at the epistemological and empirical level show the need for a more adequate theoretical framework which, besides the dimensions of meaning and rules, would also comprehend dimensions directly related to subjective life experience and to action as such.

I am not trying to re-establish either some absolute grounds of rationality or a general structure of natural needs, but to point out that action is not reducible to 'following a rule' and that the relation of action *to* rules has to be taken into account as well. One could object that the relation to rules could also be analysed in terms of 'private' rules, but in this case, as has happened to the aforementioned Boudonian concept of reason, the concept of rule would lose its specificity by becoming excessively wide. I think that in order to understand the contradictions emerging in the relation of action to rules, it is preferable to distinguish between rules, as objective codified and determinate forms, and the indeterminate character of the varied expressions of action. The relative autonomy of action with respect to meaning and to norms will have to be further analysed in the following pages, taking into account the contributions of the philosophy of praxis, phenomenology and hermeneutics.

2.3 THE REVIVAL OF THE PHILOSOPHY OF PRAXIS

The revival of the philosophy of praxis, which since 1960 has taken place mainly among German philosophers and political scientists, is rooted in the critique of neo-positivism and in the new interest in the moral and political aspects of social action.

It is well known that the concept of philosophy of praxis is directly related to Aristotle's distinction between *theoretical* and *practical* knowledge. According to Aristotle, human phenomena, being connected with decisional dimensions, cannot be analysed with the same degree of precision (*acribia*) obtainable in sciences such as theology or mathematics. Knowledge has thus to be adjusted to the nature of the object under analysis: mathematics and theology study what is *necessary* (*tò anankaion*), while ethics and politics take into consideration what is most *probable* (*tà hos epì tò poly*). Aristotle maintained that only the former forms of knowledge could reach a true scientific certainty, while the latter cannot go beyond probability.

Another meaningful Aristotelian distinction is that between instrumentally productive action, or *poiesis*, and social-practical action, or *praxis*. This latter has been particularly stressed by authors promoting the revival of the philosophy of praxis.

Criticizing Marx's overestimation of labour, Hannah Arendt has shown that, for Greek culture, the paramount activity was neither *labour* nor *production*, which, being related to biological needs, were considered as inferior slave tasks, but rather the *political* and *theoretical* activities, which, in going beyond the biological level, are connected to fame, honour and power. At this level action is no longer connected with everyday life, but acquires an exceptional and unique character (see Arendt, 1958).

In this perspective, living gestures and spoken words, which correspond to the notion of *energheia*, which Aristotle used to mean activities not orientated to a purpose or to production, were considered the greatest achievements of human beings. These activities in fact have their full meaning in themselves (see Arendt, ibid.).

The autonomous dimension of action stressed by Aristotle has been obliterated by the Western cultural tradition: all the authors who have made major contributions to reviving the philosophy of praxis (Wilhelm Hennis, Joachim Ritter, Hannah Arendt, Manfred Riedel, Ernst Vollrath) pointed out the connection established in our tradition between the priority attributed to sciences which analyse the world of *necessity* and the prevailing instrumental and teleological conception of action. The decline of political science in modern times is precisely due to the development of Cartesian rationality and empiricism and to the conception of knowledge as an *exact* science.

As a matter of fact, political science, being unable to bear comparison with scientific knowledge, has either been devalued as 'commonsense' knowledge or its object has been reduced so that it can be submitted to some measurable and rational kind of analysis. Thus human action, as an autonomous dimension different both from *poiesis* and *theory*, has not been adequately recognized. The specific characteristics of praxis, linked to liberty and to the manifold possibilities of intersubjective action, cannot in fact be interpreted in terms of 'causes' and 'principles'.

Thus we have also lost the Aristotelian dimension of *phronesis*, namely, the kind of knowledge different from theory which is more adapted to the nature of non-purposive action, since it is derived from the ethical and political relevance of practical *judgement*.

The new philosophy of praxis has also revived Kant's concept of *aesthetic judgement*, that is, the reflexive activity which connects particular with universal aspects of reality, allowing the analysis of action by following its own fundamental determinate characters: fatality, contingency, situationality, particularity (see Volpi, 1980, p. 49).

While re-evaluating some Aristotelian categories, the new philosophy of praxis has also developed some criticism of Aristotle's thought, showing that even he has mainly referred to teleological and nomotetic models and has not given enough prominence to the dimension of *phronesis*.

Demonstrating that action is not reducible to purposive rationality, the revival of the philosophy of praxis has stressed the need for a more adequate frame of reference to interpret the specific dimension of action. I shall try to show that contemporary phenomenology and hermeneutics can provide us with further elements to develop such a non-reductive approach.

2.4 LIFE-WORLD AND ANONYMOUS INTENTIONALITY

Edmund Husserl's phenomenology stresses that the individual is the bearer of a project within a meaningful world. According to the first Husserl, from *Logische Untersuchungen* to *Cartesianische Meditationen*, human experience springs from subjective intentional consciousness, a concept that Franz Brentano had formulated in his analysis of psychic phenomena and that was developed by Husserl in his *descriptive* phenomenology. Subsequently Husserlian phenomenology acquired a *transcendental* character, trying to show the constitutive dimension of *pure consciousness* as an *a priori* of individual consciousness.

Husserl's approach thus falls back on a new kind of idealism, for the origin of meaning is attributed to pure consciousness itself, whose intentional acts (*noesis*) are constitutive of the meaning of the world and its objectifications (*noema*). As Ricoeur has pointed out, the dimension of being is reduced to that of meaning, while the meaning of being is interpreted as 'intentional project' (see Ricoeur, 1969).

The general dimension of the intentionality of pure consciousness is revealed by the method of *phenomenological reduction*, based on *epoché*, that is, the suspension of judgement or a procedure which, *bracketing* notions of everyday common sense and the results of scientific knowledge, entirely alters the current attitude of human experience, and allows one 'to go back to things themselves', by freeing the original intuitive potentialities of consciousness. Through this method human experience appears as unitary organizational activity, prior to any specific point of view: it is with reference to this background that the different concrete experiences of individuals can be explained (see Fink, 1966).

The different levels of reality (level of material things submitted to causal laws; level of the animal world submitted to instincts; level of psychic reality characterized by motivations) can be considered as the result of the constitutive activity of transcendental consciousness. Similarly, society and culture are not *given* to consciousness but are constructed by it.

According to Husserl, the possibility of shared meanings and co-operative action – that is, of language, society, history – is based on transcendental intersubjectivity which is at the origin of all psychic reality. However, in one of his last works, Husserl, after reading Heidegger's *Being and Time*, extends his analysis to everyday life practices: *The Crisis of European Sciences and Transcendental Phenomenology*, published posthumously in 1959, is an interpretation of contemporary society based on the critique of the reductivism of positivistic science. Husserl points out that, by absolutizing the practical-empirical dimension orientated to welfare, positivistic science tends to reduce man himself to a thing and obliterates the problems that are more important for him: the problem of the sense and non-sense of human life as a whole (see Husserl, 1959).

By its rigorous objectivism, positivistic science disregards the subjective dimension and shatters knowledge by reducing it merely to the ascertainment of facts and to mathematical measurements. According to Husserl, it is necessary to re-establish, through 'a heroism of reason definitely overcoming naturalism', the general intentionality which was at the origin of philosophical thought, and to rediscover the intersubjective meaning which orientates social life, history and the ethical ideals of humanity (see Husserl, ibid.).

In order to achieve this aim we must go back to the *life-world* (*Lebenswelt*), that is, to the ground of human life where we 'live intuitively with the world's realities as they are', drawing from the 'simple experience' of subjective life in its pre-predicative, pre-scientific character. Thus the subjective-relational dimension which founds, in the last analysis, any objective reality is no longer hidden as in the objectivistic approach of positivistic science. The life-world is in fact interpreted by Husserl as 'the realm of first evidences', as the source of sense for any determinate life reality.

In this perspective Husserl formulates his concept of *anonymous intentionality*, that is, the set of those conceptual intentions through which something is put into reality, something of which no one is aware, which no one assumes as his own, but nevertheless influences everybody. Subjective consciousness is thus no longer conceived of only as an active principle, but also as the result of a wider meaning connected with life itself. The individual, as a product of the life-world, appears as a finite reality within an historical horizon, although there is always the possibility that subjective consciousness will distance itself from and innovate the determinate historical forms.

The constitutive historicity of the individual, the fact that he belongs to the life-world before being aware of himself or of things surrounding him, is the first step in understanding why action is not reducible to meaning or to the symbolic-normative order. In this perspective the Cartesian *cogito* appears in fact to be no longer the origin of any foundation of certainty, and the interpreter becomes aware that he himself is part of the reality that has to be interpreted. Along these lines, understanding can be analysed as a *way of being* of the subject, and an *ontology of understanding* can be developed, challenging the priority attributed in Western philosophical tradition to the epistemological dimension.

2.5 THE ONTOLOGY OF UNDERSTANDING AND THE HERMENEUTIC CIRCLE

Ricoeur has pointed out that Heidegger's ontological research puts an end to the characteristic 'predominance of epistemology' of Dilthey's hermeneutics. Dilthey was above all interested in establishing the autonomy of the 'sciences of the spirit' in their relation to the 'sciences of nature'. Through the distinction between *understanding* and *explanation* and by stressing the capacity of the individual to empathically grasp the psychological experience of others, Dilthey wanted above all to guarantee both the specificity and the equal dignity of the historical and social sciences (see Ricoeur, 1987). In Dilthey, however, the rationalistic and positivistic conception of science is still predominant, and the 'sciences of the spirit' are also mainly conceived with reference to that model. Thus for Dilthey understanding still has priority over being.

Heidegger, on the contrary, stressed the ontological dimension by considering the nature of the human subject as a *being who questions about Being*. In the latter perspective, understanding is interpreted as 'a distinctive character of being as being-in-the-world' (Ricoeur, ibid.). The connection between being-in-the-world and the cognitive and interpretative activity of the individual thus becomes evident. In *Sein und Zeit*, *Dasein* is considered as *thrown* into the world, as involved from the beginning in the existential situation characterized by affectivity, anxiety and care (*Sorge*), but at the same time the *Dasein* is also capable of *project* and *decision* (see Heidegger, 1927).

The involvement of *Dasein* in the existential situation shows the pre-predicative character of our relation to the world, the existential fore-structure anticipating all cognition and self-awareness. It is precisely from this fore-structure that action develops as a dimension directly connected with being-in-the-world, *prior* to any conscious understanding or interpretation.

The situation into which the individual is pro-jected is characterized by reflexive comprehension, but the latter is deeply conditioned by the situation itself, that is, by that pre-predicative relation to what is ready-to-hand (*zuhanden*) which is already in itself a form of understanding and interpretation (see Heidegger, 1927). The Heideggerian concept of fore-structure is, as Derrida has pointed out, an essential dimension referring to the fact that the individual is from the beginning *engagé*, involved, in a situation *before* making any conscious choice (see Derrida, 1987, p. 153).

Truth in this perspective is no longer conceived of, as in Descartes, as a transparent rational construction, but as a revealing *event* emerging from the relation between understanding and situational conditions. Consciousness and its object are no longer considered as separate dimensions, but as moments of the same process of construction of reality both in its subjective and objective aspects.

The fundamental role of the concept of the *hermeneutic circle* is thus evident: the meaning anticipated by the interpreter is part of the meaning to be interpreted, that is, the interpreter is part of what is to be interpreted. As Heidegger has pointed out, the hermeneutic circle is not a vicious circle but is, rather, the acknowledgement of the fore-structure proper to being-in-the-world: a recognition opening up new possibilities of original insights.

The reference to the hermeneutic circle shows: (a) that understanding itself is a way of being of *Dasein*; and (b) that the being of the latter is constituted by *care* (*Sorge*), that is, that the individual is from the beginning involved in taking care of himself and of things in the world.

Gadamer has developed his critique of Enlightenment along these same lines, by pointing out that there is no knowledge without *prejudice*. Hermeneutic experience is, in fact, above all the acknowledgement of our belonging to an historical tradition and a language. The concept of *awareness of effective history* (*wirkungsgeschichtliches Bewusstsein*) is directly connected with Heidegger's notion of pre-understanding. The latter, as Ricoeur has observed, shows that the conditions of any discourse can neither be entirely controlled nor entirely transparent: the essentially historical character of those conditions explains the impossibility of a totally clear reflexivity (see Ricoeur, 1987, p. 91).

The hermeneutic approach thus shows that the interpretation of reality is part of a more complex process connected with a pre-scientific and more original understanding of the world, such understanding being always already mediated by a cultural tradition and a linguistic community (*Gesprächgemeinschaft*). This means that there is always something left unsaid in any discourse and that a total explanation is impossible (see Ricoeur, ibid., p. 93).

If Heidegger's and Gadamer's approaches are very similar on this point, it is also possible to find some common ground between their concept of pre-understanding and Wittgenstein's relation of language-games to forms of life. As Ricoeur has pointed out, the classic metaphysics, the Cartesian subject and the Kantian concept of 'thing itself' stand here, for both Heidegger and Wittgenstein, as common enemies. On the contrary, what divides them is the fact that language-games theory cannot analyse its own pre-conditions. If any discourse is from the beginning already involved in a language-game it is not possible to analyse the linguistic condition in itself. In order to achieve this analysis it is necessary to establish the game of language (in this case the game of philosophy) in an understanding of being-in-the-world prior to any game of language. However, it is also true that even Wittgenstein refers to a *natural* language as the basis for and horizon of any understanding of meaning (see Ricoeur, ibid., pp. 97–8).

As I have already suggested, Heidegger's and Gadamer's preunderstanding, stressing the involvement of the individual in a situation prior to any reflexivity and interpretation, allows recognition of the real dimension of action. Being connected with the complexity of a pre-given situation, the latter appears as a dimension which can never be exhaustively understood. As Heidegger observed, *Dasein* is not only what is nearest to us, but also what is most distant from us (Heidegger, 1927). Similarly action, although it is an expression of what we are, is at the same time that which is most difficult for us to comprehend.

The theory of social action has not till now adequately exploited the consequences deriving from the acknowledgement that action emerges in a pre-linguistic and pre-reflexive situation, characterized by affectivity and care. On the contrary, in the last few years there has been a tendency to consider hermeneutics only with reference to language and symbolic order, thus removing the specific ontological dimension of Heidegger's thought.

As is well known, even Heidegger, after the *Kehre*, progressively abandoned the phenomenological analysis of the existential situation, seeking in poetical language a different way of referring to Being. This turning point in Heidegger's thought may be justified by the aim of thinking of Being as independent from *Dasein*, thus minimizing the subjective decisionist dimension developed in *Sein und Zeit* within the problem of life authenticity. Nevertheless, the validity for the sociological theory of action of the phenomenological analysis of *Dasein* by the first Heidegger should not be put into question.

Gadamer too has stressed the essentially linguistic character of being-in-the-world, thus weakening the tension between the pre-linguistic and the linguistic dimensions of the existential situation. But it is also true that in Gadamer, as in Heidegger, language always has an ontological character: language *reveals* and at the same time *conceals* Being, language brings Being in itself, but it is also what *alludes* (*Winke*) to Being, thus showing that language is not commensurate with Being itself.

The relation to tradition still has in Gadamer that dimension of ontological belonging, which both Apel and Habermas tend to obliterate, by stressing the critical attitude towards tradition and by establishing the priority of communicative procedures as a basis of formal rationality. Subjective experience is submitted by Habermas to the criteria of communicative rationality and to the validity claims proper to an ideal linguistic situation. In so doing Habermas re-establishes the priority of transcendental reflexivity on existential situation and, as mentioned above, reduces life-world to a merely cultural or communicative reality.

The opposition between Gadamer and Habermas is based precisely on the different relevance attributed to the ontological dimension of pre-understanding with regard to that of reflexivity and communication. If Gadamer's attitude towards this aspect at times appears to be ambivalent, in his approach there is still the possibility of recognizing the essential limits of language in its relation to Being. To consider language as a fundamental ontological horizon does not necessarily mean that language can exhaust the entire reality. According to Gadamer, the historical being-in-the-world, although it dwells in language, is never as such revealed by language: the historical being remains hidden in language since the nature of language itself remains essentially unknown to us (see Gadamer, 1971b). It thus shows that Gadamer thinks of language in terms of a reality having the same elusive character of Being, that is, in terms quite different from Habermas's analytical approach to language and the current philosophy of language. Gadamer's reference to the reductive character of language is even more explicit when he states that if 'Being that can be understood *is* language' not all Being can be understood. Gadamer also stresses that the awareness of effective-history is 'unavoidably more being than consciousness' and that self-knowledge can never be complete: this shows that life experience always transcends understanding (see Gadamer, 1972, pp. 352, 536).

Habermas instead refers to communicative rationality as a deep structure emerging once the coercions and distortions of the authority of tradition are eliminated. Reflexivity can be released from its connection with tradition, and thus becomes an autonomous principle of orientation. By referring to an ideal model of rational transparency which overcomes every contradiction with a free communicative exchange, the Habermasian approach appears to be a new, more sophisticated version of the Utopia of freedom from any coercion and conflict thanks to self-evident reason. Even if, when stressing the function of the critique of ideology, Habermas implicitly recognizes the relevance of the capacity of *negation* specific to subjective consciousness, when he tries to found rationality positively by reducing the pre-predicative structure of life-world to a merely cultural dimension, he falls into a sort of absolutization of the communicative structure. This attitude is obviously antithetic to Heidegger's and Gadamer's hermeneutics, and also, at least in certain aspects, to Wittgenstein's language-games theory. All these last approaches stress in one way or another the limitations of understanding and the priority of experience as compared to the forms of rationality.

In order to remain in the hermeneutic perspective, it is necessary, on the one hand, to recognize that life experience is not exhausted by the linguistic dimension, although not ignoring the constitutive character of language for the construction of reality; on the other hand, as well as our belonging to tradition and the Husserlian 'natural experience of life' (*Lebensfahrung*), it is also necessary to stress the capacity of the individual to negate the cultural objectivations, thus becoming open to ever-new forms of life experience.

The last issue can be developed from Gadamer's concept of experience as an initial *experience of nonentity*, that is, the perception that things 'are not as we thought they were' and the development of self-consciousness as a unit through the acknowledgement of what is alien to it. This happens mainly through the distinction between the horizon of the past and that of present: the *fusion of horizons*, according to Gadamer's terminology, becomes in fact possible, thanks to the awareness that we are alien to the past and, at the same time, thanks to our capacity to establish a relation with the past through the specific interpretative horizon of our time (see Gadamer, 1972, p. 356).

Thus the connection with tradition also allows a dialectic approach which, through the fusion of horizons, creates ever-new perspectives:

> Experience as such can never be merely knowledge... true experience is always a reference to the possibility of new experiences. When we consider somebody as an 'expert', we never consider only that he has become such through the experiences he has *made*, but also we imply that he is *open* to new experiences. (Gadamer, 1972, p. 411)

The expert is essentially an *undogmatic* person capable of learning from experience: 'The dialectic of experience does not end with acquired knowledge, but with that opening to experience which is a product of experience itself' (Gadamer, ibid.).

An essential feature of experience is the capacity to release oneself from the prison of established things through a sort of *dis-location* which, by involving the actor in the game of action, puts him 'out of himself' (see Vattimo, 1981, pp. 72–3).

Experience also means the acknowledgement of human limitedness, of the fact that we are not in control of time, that our capacity to predict is limited and our projects always uncertain and, above all, that *'the question always prevails on the answer'*. In this same perspective we have also to consider the experience of the other as a *thou*, as the capacity to 'listen to his appeal and let it lead us' (Gadamer, 1972, pp. 417–18).

The notion of subjectivity based on Heidegger's concept of *Dasein*, as being which is not only *thrown* into life but which, through understanding, projects its own possibilities of being (*Entwurf*), appears as an essential dimension of hermeneutic. If it is true that both Heidegger and Gadamer give pre-eminence to *Sein* (Being) over *Bewusstsein* (consciousness) (see Da Re, 1982, p. 47), it is also true that Heidegger's critique of the conception of Being as mere presence is at the basis of the radical rejection, with constant reference to the 'difference' of Being, of any absolutization of the contingent objectivations of the present. Similarly, Gadamer's recognition of the limitations of language is at the basis of the essential capacity to negate the constituted orders and open up ever-new possibilities.

As I have already pointed out, the *fusion of horizons* becomes possible thanks to the awareness of the difference between past and present. In spite of the fact that the awareness of effective-history is 'more Being than consciousness', the latter, according to Gadamer, is also what allows one to escape ideological rigidity and 'to freely decide about the soundness or unsoundness of my pre-understanding'. In this way the unavoidable prejudices determining my pre-understanding can be transformed: the capacity to develop new pre-understandings through any information available, explains the relentless strength of experience. The aim of hermeneutics is to bring knowledge from its false objectivations back to its hermeneutical foundations (see Gadamer, 1971b).

Beside the initial dimension of *belonging* to tradition, in Gadamerian hermeneutics there is thus the possibility of a critical *distantiation* from the objectivated forms. It is precisely with reference to the oscillation between distantiation and belonging, stressed by Ricoeur, that we shall be better able to understand the ambivalent character of the dynamic relationship between action and symbolic order.

2.6 EXISTENTIAL PHENOMENOLOGY AND HERMENEUTICS

Paul Ricoeur's critical analysis of the relation between existential phenomenology and hermeneutics has given an important contribution to the understanding of the specific character of social action in its relation to symbolic-normative order.

Our comprehension of social action develops through the analysis of the forms of expression (language, social representations and so on) and of the cultural documents or 'texts' into which life experience is objectivated. However, in its connection with phenomenology, hermeneutics is never merely a semantic analysis of meaning. When language is considered only semantically as a closed self-referential system, the fundamental function of the sign, the fact that it *stands for* something else, that it is *allusive*, is forgotten: 'Language in itself, as a meaningful system, has to be referred to existence' (Ricoeur, 1969, p. 29).

Ricoeur considers the symbolic order to be a structure of significance where a *direct, primary, literal* meaning refers to another *indirect, secondary, figured* meaning which can be apprehended only through the first. For this reason hermeneutics is not merely an *epistemology* of interpretation, but also an *ontology* of understanding: the comprehension of the symbolic multivalent expressions is always an interpretation of life experience and the Self.

The individual who develops, through signs and symbols, a reflexive interpretation of himself is in the hermeneutic perspective no longer considered as the Cartesian subject establishing in the *Cogito* an immediate relation with himself; it is, rather, somebody who, through the exegesis of his life, discovers that he has been put into being *before* any self-consciousness (see Ricoeur, 1969, p. 33).

In this same perspective Ricoeur makes a distinction between the *semantic* level, where interpretation is considered as the recognition of the different levels of significance and as decoding hidden meanings, and a *reflexive* level where, presupposing the need to refer language to existence, the connection between signs and comprehension of Self is established.

As was stressed by Marx, Nietzsche and Freud, 'immediate' consciousness is mainly a 'false' consciousness: reflexivity is above all a critique of false consciousness, following the principle 'to lose Self in order to find Ego'. Consequently reflexivity appears to be *doubly indirect*, as, on the one hand, existence can be grasped only through texts or documents and, on the other hand, immediate consciousness is false (see Ricoeur, 1969, p. 31).

On these presuppositions, hermeneutics is released from the traditional foundation of subjectivity and 'restored' in the existential dimension of *desire*. Taking into account the relevance of the relation between meaning and desire, sense and energy, language and life for Freud, we can understand, according to Ricoeur, that the individual, far from being self-sufficient and self-founding, is *thrown* into being. By deciphering the illusions of desire we can go deeper into the relation between reflexivity and meaning; although, as I have already said, we can never get directly to desire, but only through the interpretation of signs and symbols (see Ricoeur, 1969, p. 33).

The fact that desire has to be guessed 'behind the enigmas of consciousness' without ever being grasped in itself, stops one falling into a sort of 'mythology of pulsions' and shows the difference between hermeneutics and any form of vitalism.

With Ricoeur's approach to the authentic meaning of hermeneutics we can clarify the context of a non-reductive theory of action. It is essential for this purpose to distinguish between the objectivated forms of symbolic mediation constitutive of the 'texts' of life which are susceptible of structural analysis, and the existential dimension whose recognition, although it is always indirect and partial, cannot be avoided. Existence is, in fact, as mentioned above, a constant reference of the symbolic order. Only by recognizing the tension internal to this reference can one give due attention to the contradictions of social action. Although he stresses the autonomy of the text and the possibility of considering an accomplished action as text, Ricoeur conceives of the structural analysis of the text only as part of the wider interpretative process which, in the last analysis, has to be referred to the existential dimension of action (see Ricoeur, 1986, p. 183).

If we can analyse action empirically through its objectivated forms or *traces*, we must not forget that action is also an *event*: from a theoretical standpoint it is important to take into account that any fixing of an event (written text as compared to live talk, 'traces' as compared to actual action, and so on) implies a certain loss (see Ricoeur, 1985, p. 171). Ricoeur's concept of trace as an 'effect-sign' refers to the meaningful relation between action as an event and the signs it has left. In the latter perspective the connection, stressed by Ricoeur, between action and desire allows us, as will become clear in the next chapter, to take into account the many symbolic meanings of social action.

Ricoeur's distinction between *belonging* (*appartenance*) and *distantiation* is also relevant to the theory of action. This distinction in fact corresponds to that between *identification to* and *negation of* the objectivated forms which we have already considered to be a capacity of consciousness.

With reference to the foundation of the critique of ideology, Ricoeur correctly stresses the dialectic character of the relation between the experience of belonging to a tradition or a socio-cultural context and the experience of distantiation, that is, of becoming estranged (*Verfremdung*) from that same tradition or context (Ricoeur, 1986, p. 365). Without expounding here the analysis of Ricoeur's theory, I shall only recall that his distinction fits into the controversy over Gadamer, accused of ontologizing hermeneutics to the point of giving pre-eminence to historical tradition on judgement, and Habermas's critical approach which instead gives pre-eminence to rational reflexivity on any historical conditioning.

Ricoeur's attempt is correctly orientated to avoid both extremes: on the one hand, of stressing the individual's dependence on historical–cultural tradition to the point of denying any possibility of dissent from the prevailing social order (as even hermeneutics would appear dependent on it); and, on the other hand, of univocally stressing the dimension of distantiation, thus falling into a new form of idealism by assuming, as in Habermas's theory of communicative rationality, the possibility of judging the contextual relativity of interpretations from a superior point of view free from any connection with tradition. The first issue removes the negative dimension of distantiation, while the second tends to ignore the fundamental hermeneutic assumption that being-in-the-world is prior to consciousness and knowledge.

Only by taking into account the radical limit due to the unavoidable dependence of our understanding on tradition and prejudices, can one correctly establish a critique of the different objectivated forms. In fact, that critique develops from the impossibility of considering the definite reductive forms of symbolic mediation as absolute truth and, at the same time, from the awareness that these forms, precisely because they are definite, ever tend to assume an absolute character. In this context the critique of ideology appears, in the last analysis, to be the recognition of the unavoidable 'ideological' character of any form of representation and interpretation of reality (see Crespi, 1987; see also Chapter Five, section 5.1).

Distantiation is thus eminently *negative*, as it does not lead to an absolute overcoming of prejudices but to their transformation through the gradual shifting from one form of interpretation to another. In this way neither of those forms can be dogmatically confirmed, thus becoming functional to political power. Seeking its own absolute legitimation, political power in fact always uses ideological forms which are not recognized as such.

When distantiation is considered instead as a *positive* capacity for giving up prejudices and developing 'non-ideological' forms, there is then the risk of falling into a form of ideology precisely because the attribution of priority to knowledge pretends to establish an entirely non-ideological point of view.

Hermeneutics is essentially awareness of the 'incomprehensible within comprehension' (Ripanti, 1979, p. 15), or of what Gadamer indicates as the 'inconclusiveness of any comprehension and historical reflection'. In the hermeneutic perspective there is no transparency of meaning, nor is any 'exclusive possession of the true opinion' possible; communication is therefore conceived as a 'reciprocal testing of different prejudices' (Gadamer, 1971b, pp. 301, 305).

Ricoeur's theory of the dialectic relation between belonging and distantiation shows that the recognition of the impact of tradition and prejudices on our understanding does not necessarily lead to a blind submission to prevailing sociocultural orders. As Gadamer has pointed out, all change, as well as all attitudes opposed to change, inevitably takes place in relation to tradition. That dialectic, which corresponds to the aforementioned relation between identification to and negation of the objectivated forms, shows the social actor as both a *product* and an active *producer* of social reality.

2.7 HERMENEUTICS AND PRAGMATISM

In trying to develop a new approach to pragmatism, the American philosopher Richard Rorty has recently compared the theoretical perspectives of John Dewey and Martin Heidegger, and stressed some common points between the two who, because of their cultural backgrounds and general orientations, have always been considered quite distant from each other (see Rorty, 1982, p. 67).

Without entering fully into the problem of the legitimacy of Rorty's approach, I think we must recognize that, at least to a certain extent, the comparison between hermeneutics and pragmatism can be useful for the theory of action. Here I shall mention only very briefly some general aspects of the question, which can be taken as starting points for further research.

A first element common to both hermeneutics and pragmatism, which, for the latter, is related to the different positions of Charles Peirce, William James and John Dewey, is the critique of metaphysics and positivism. Both hermeneutics and pragmatism emphasize that knowledge develops from a concrete sociocultural situation and from the practical experience of the individual in his relation to his environment and to other individuals. The similarity of both approaches on this point is indubitable, even if the same result is achieved from very different epistemological perspectives. Developing Peirce's logical theory of meaning, William James pointed out that the relation between subject and object, between consciousness and external reality, had to be considered as an interactive process between dimensions that could not be kept separate. Referring to the tendency of classical empiricism to consider knowledge as a mirror of nature, James stressed the active character of knowledge as a capacity for finding out ever-new hypotheses. Defining truth in terms of satisfactory adaptation to reality, James did not conceive of adaptation as general correspondence between our ideas and external reality but as the capacity to establish a specific functional relation with our environment. This relation was in turn conceived of as a result not only of the adherence to the concrete conditions of the situation, but also of the transforming activity specific to the intentional project of the individual.

The active character of knowledge in its close relation to praxis is also stressed by Dewey's 'humanistic naturalism'. Pointing out the temporal dimension of knowledge and criticizing both materialistic determinism and the passive conception of sensibility, Dewey considers knowledge as a process developing in an interactive field, where practical experience has a constitutive function. Far from being merely a mirror of reality, knowledge, according to Dewey, appears as the controlled and orientated transformative process going from an indeterminate to a determinate situation, and unifying into a whole the different original elements (see Dewey, 1938, p. 104).

The fact that knowledge is the reduction of complexity and mediation, and must then be conceived of as an active selection and transformation of immediate data, is thus evidenced by Dewey. In this context the cognitive achievements are never considered as permanent and definite truths, but rather as hypotheses giving support to action, or as instruments whose functional validity has to be tested again each time with reference to their practical consequences.

Assigning to philosophy the task of overcoming the division between practical routine and experimental intellect, Dewey criticizes the traditional separation between theory and praxis, and stresses their interrelation in the processes which actively transform reality. If theory orientates praxis, the latter in turn, by challenging the established scientific procedures and the codified social patterns, also has a function in the cognitive process.

Thus, for both hermeneutics and pragmatism, knowledge is an interpretative process which, starting from historical concrete contexts and intersubjective practical experience, leads to results continuously susceptible of revision: the priority of being-in-the-world on understanding appears to be confirmed by pragmatism, which is also orientated to consider action both in its connection with the conditions of the historical and social situation and as a creative dimension.

But for the pragmatic experience that I have mentioned here, the most important contribution to the sociological theory of action was given by George Mead's analysis of the relation between 'I' and 'me'. Although he defines his theory as 'social behaviorism', Mead criticized the reductionism of the behaviouristic approach. According to this author, the behaviour that may be described has always an internal dimension also, not separated from the external manifestation of action. In fact, Mead considered Wilhelm Wundt's theory of the parallelism between corporeal events or processes of the central nervous system and psychical experiences of consciousness, and maintained that the theory was inadequate to explain the genesis of ideas and the subject itself. While Wundt had considered the subjective Self to be prior to the communicative social processes, Mead thought that Selves had to be explained with reference to the social process and the primary phenomenon of communication (Mead, 1934, p. 69). In this perspective Mead, as is well known, gave essential relevance to *gesture* as an elementary phenomenon of communication, specific to the animal as well as to the human world.

In the animal world the gesture (for example, a dog's growl) is at the same time an outer and an inner attitude; but being simply a response to a stimulus, the latter is neither conscious nor intentional. Such reactive behaviours are also present in the human world but, according to Mead, the human gesture tends to become an expression of symbolic meaning and intentional will also: gesture then becomes *language*. If initially the function of gesture allows a mutual automatic adjustment between different individuals, the conscious and meaningful communication, developing mainly through language, guarantees conditions of adjustment and readjustment which are much more adequate than the automatic gesture.

The reflexive interiorization of the outer gesture and its transformation in symbolic meaning show that cognition and the individual's relation with himself emerge within a shared social meaning or against the background of a general frame of reference defined by Mead as 'the generalised Other'. Social interaction is always the basis of common sense, but the symbolic gesture or language, and the consciousness which is structurally linked to it, allow us to select meanings and control social communication: this capacity is defined by Mead as *Mind*. The latter is not merely an inner structure of the individual but, rather, the result of an interactive and symbolically mediated process.

In the same manner, the individual Self also develops initially through concrete relations with others. In the first phase of life, it develops by organizing the specific attitudes of others towards him or themselves within concrete social relations (family, peer group, ethnic groups and the rest). In the second phase the individual organizes not only the particular individual attitudes but also the social attitudes of the 'generalised Other' (the social group considered as a whole). The individual's self-image is thus the product of his social experience and the symbolic forms mediating that experience.

In this perspective, Mead stressed the function of play for the construction of Self. In the first years of life, the child tends to assume different roles by imitating those of adults in spontaneous *play*. At this level, as Mead pointed out, the child has not yet a fully formed Self, for he is not yet able to organize life as a whole but, rather, lives the different roles he assumes in a split way. Successively the individual learns *games*, that is, how to play in groups by following some common rules and thus assuming different roles within an organized system of actions and reactions. Thus the child ends up by perceiving himself as a unit, objectivating his own Self through the mediation of the image of Self which others send back to him.

The attitude of the social community or the 'generalised Other' towards individual personality and the control exercised by the same community on members' behaviours thus appear to be essentially influencing the type of relation the individual has with himself. However, the individual is not merely a passive product of the social process, but is also an active source of change and innovation.

As Mead pointed out, two distinct dimensions make up the Self: *me* and *I*. It has been remarked (see Lewis, 1979) that Mead's conception of the 'I' has some ambiguity and can be subject to different interpretations. But this ambiguity is explicitly recognized by Mead himself when he observes that the 'I' 'lies beyond the range of immediate experience' (Mead, 1934, p. 140): there cannot be a precise definition of the 'I' as such. If 'me' is the organized unit of social codified *attitudes*, the 'I' is the *response* to these attitudes, the typical individual reaction to the socially organized 'me'.

In making a distinction between 'I' and 'me' Mead seems to recognize implicitly the dynamic between *identity* ('me') and *non-identity* ('I') that I defined above as the negative capacity specific of consciousness. The 'I', as an active and relatively autonomous response to the codified attitudes of 'me' as a social product, has a creative character: 'reducing to a minimum' the conventional form of 'me', the 'I' can actively introduce changes in society itself (see Mead, 1934, pp. 218ff., 326).

Even though intimately connected with pragmatism, Mead had also studied with Dilthey and was 'familiar with the latter's intellectual aims' (Joas, 1985, p. 41): his experience thus appears to be the intersecting point between pragmatism and the tradition which is at the origin of contemporary hermeneutics. This explains why Mead has made an important contribution to a better understanding of the relation between action and cognition, between action and the determined forms of symbolic-normative mediation.

Pragmatism has also evidenced dimensions that risk being overlooked by the hermeneutic perspective. I am referring particularly to the practical problem of founding a social project which, denying any absolutization of the forms of the symbolic-normative order and social institutions, would develop beyond any abstract scheme as a capacity for *attention* to concrete situations, and of *dealing* with their unavoidable contradictions.

In this same direction one could give way to a *non-reductive pragmatism*, since the tendentially instrumental character of the pragmatic attitude can expand by reference to the indeterminate dimensions and changing requirements of life experience, stressing the creative potentialities of action. Thus it is evident that the priority given to the negative dimension of consciousness by no means excludes the possibility of a positive social project. The critique of the established social order can develop concretely only through a constructive proposal based on the evaluation of the contingent situation and the selection of its actual possibilities.

The connection between the negative dimension of consciousness and the positive social project eliminates from the latter every character of voluntaristic imposition. Making concrete choices with an awareness of the unavoidably reductive character of any selection, the social project thus appears to be qualified by the constant capacity of reflexive adjustment through trial and error. Thus the *violence* done to reality which, at least to a certain extent, is implied in every reduction of complexity or determinate form of interpretation, would be attenuated.

In this same perspective, the pragmatic dimension, as we shall see later (Chapter Four), is also constitutive of the function of power, understood as the capacity to deal with the contradictions emerging in the relation between determinacy and indeterminacy.

By discussing aspects of the philosophy of praxis, phenomenology, hermeneutics and pragmatism, we have been able to identify some conceptual categories which clarify the specific character of action.

The priority of being-in-the-world over cognition shows that action is involved in historical experience before being aware of its motivations and of the rules orientating it. Action is thus revealed as an 'ontological' as well as a psychological and symbolic reality.

The recognition that action is not reducible to meaning, the rules of communication or the symbolic-normative order, allows us to take into account the fundamental contradictions of social action in its relation to the structures of the social system along the above-mentioned lines of identification ('belonging') and distantiation, identity and non-identity. It also shows that the practical necessity of dealing with those contradictions is a fundamental drive of social action as such.

In this perspective sociology appears to be grounded on the observation of concrete social action through some general categories. First, action should be interpreted with reference to the contradictions of being-in-the-world that the social actor must face each time within the different forms of historical and social contingency. Secondly, action should be interpreted with reference to the structural and material as well as the cultural conditions of the specific situation considered.

In the next chapter I shall try to develop the analysis of the general categories specific to the ambivalent relation between action and the determinate forms of symbolic-normative mediation.

3

General Categories of Action

'If, for a thousand years, one would ask Life why it lives, and Life could answer, it would only say: I live because I live.'

M. Eckhart

The ontological dimension of action shows that the latter is reducible neither to conscious intentionality nor to meaning or rules. Thus action has an undetermined character which has to be taken into account in order to understand the essentially contradictory nature of social dynamics.

On the basis of these presuppositions, several general categories of life experience from which action emerges can be identified. As meta-theoretical references they supply a general background for the specific hypotheses orientating the empirical analysis of social action.

3.1 ACTION AND DESIRE

With reference to the aforementioned distinction between behaviour and action, the latter appears to be strictly linked to the reflexivity of consciousness or to that way of being which is characterized by questioning about the meaning of its own being-there. The specific questioning of the reflexive experience creates a distance between the actor and his own objective reality, revealing a sort of *void* or *lack of being* that, in the final analysis, is never to be fulfilled.

Need refers to a physical or psychological necessity connected to the survival of the individual in his relation to the natural and social environment. Need as such is, in principle, always susceptible of being fulfilled. *Desire* instead, as a dimension emerging in the void opened by the questioning of the individual about his own being, is by definition always unfulfilled.

Only a self-creating being could, in fact, give himself an adequate reason for his being there but, as mentioned above, the being-in-the-world is thrown into a situation that he has not chosen; therefore, he will never be able, except with the help of some god, to give himself an exhaustive explanation of his own being. In this sense, action originally emerges 'with no reason' in a context irreducible to principles, causes or teleological perspectives: no individual free from the will to power or manipulation will think of himself as able to fix absolute principles or ends to action, which is in its origin *an-archic* (see Schürmann, 1982).

The concept of desire not only presupposes an original situation of indeterminacy, open to the possibility of asking questions about being, but also presupposes that the individual will deeply perceive this indeterminacy as a deprivation which should be fulfilled at any cost. Throughout centuries of human history this experience has been interpreted in many fashions, but here we shall simply take it as a factual presupposition.

Nevertheless, one could ask if, instead of being a universal category, the *feeling* of the original void were not a *cultural* phenomenon, connected with particular historical contexts. I think one should answer this by making a distinction between the *awareness* or the *way of expressing* the feeling of emptiness, which is undoubtedly of a cultural type, and the fact that *every* culture is seemingly characterized by the attempt to control, by different kinds of 'answers' and 'repressions', the dimension of indeterminacy connected with the experience, both conscious or unconscious, of emptiness and desire.

When compared to the instinctual state of the animal, strictly connected with the structure of biological needs, desire appears to be the result of the weakening of the instinctual mechanisms and of the consequent character of indeterminacy assumed by the natural *drives*; since they are no longer strictly orientated to functional or natural purposes, the latter, in Freud's words, have become *polymorphous* and *polyvalent*.

As Freud pointed out, the function of the symbolic-normative order is precisely to replace the instinctual system by a set of determined outlets guiding the unconscious drives towards non-destructive solutions for the individual and society. However, the relation between the indeterminacy of the drives, or in Freudian terms the id, and the determinacy of the forms of symbolic-normative mediation, covers an intermediate level that, following Lacan, I shall call the *Imaginary* (*Imaginaire*).

The Imaginary is the meeting point between unconscious drives and symbolic forms at a level where the symbolic meaning still has a high degree of indeterminacy: even at this level the symbolic forms have an historical origin, but in this case they are freely used according to the unconscious 'logic' of the drives. The Imaginary develops as fantasy or *dream*, both night- and daydreaming. In both cases dream can be confused with *reality*, but generally only daydreams can be collectively shared.

Deriving its strength from the drives of 'id', desire initially meets meaning within the Imaginary, which offers the former a great many illusory rewards since it is not linked to the principle of reality; on the other hand, the more codified symbolic-normative order, as a product of complexity reduction, offers a limited set of effective possibilities of expression, which are considered *real*. The symbolic-normative order is, in fact, grounded on socially shared meanings, functional as such to individual and collective survival.

According to this perspective, the relation between unconscious and reality can be perceived as a continuum starting from the id, or polymorphous unconscious drives, passing through the *Imaginary* and *Symbolic* and finally reaching *Reality*, or the historical product of collective experience mediated by the symbolic-normative forms.

As is well known, the categories of Imaginary, Symbolic and Reality have been used by Jacques Lacan in his psychoanalytic theory which, in some of its essential aspects, was directly influenced by Heidegger's thought. According to Lacan, the fact that the void (*manque*) originating being-in-the-world will never be filled, is hidden by desire, for the latter appears as a capacity to fancy the Thing (*la Chose*), that is, the absolute imaginary object which will entirely fulfil desire as such.

Nevertheless, desire does not only involve the Imaginary but also the Symbolic and Reality and, in its absolutizing logic orientated to a total fulfilment, it uses them through *sublimation*, namely, the process by which *partial* objects are assumed as *absolute* (see Lacan, 1986, p. 105).

Freud's and Lacan's conceptual categories are all the more relevant to the theory of social action because they stress the undetermined character of desire and its capacity to entrust any object with symbolic meaning.

As energy developing from the original emptiness, desire is more than anything a *will to be*. This explains why desire is always 'desire for the Other', desire for what we don't have, desire we imagine the Other has. Thus, desire is always a 'second-degree' desire; that is, it is not only a desire symbolically mediated, but is also in itself always a *symbol* of something else: 'the demand is always a demand of something else and in every fulfilment of a need it requires something else' (Lacan, 1986, p. 340).

Desire is absolute and infinite: *nothing* can fulfil it except the fulness of being, which is precisely what was irreparably endangered by the reflexivity of consciousness, which broke the natural unity and created a distance between the individual and the world – the individual and his Self. The fulness of being can then only be the product of imagination: through symbolic meanings desire gets hold of partial objects and sublimates them as the *Thing* ('the fulness of being'), that is, it gets hold of objects which it does *not* actually desire.

In this context even the principle of *primum vivere* appears to be undetermined, as almost everything can supply the illusion of 'being alive'. Even interdiction, seemingly the opposite of desire, is actually a product of desire itself. In fact, according to Lacan, desire is at the origin of the law formulated in the symbolic order. The interdiction gives determinacy to desire and supplies that certitude sought by desire: 'in the fact that man has a sense of duty, there is often nothing else than fear of the risks of unpredictability if these duties were lacking' (Lacan, 1986, p. 354).

For the theory of social action it is most important to take into account the capacity of desire to transform objects into symbols, as well as the fact that there are no necessary links between desire and those objects. It thus seems that any social action is also always the *symbol* of something else, and that the meaning of that symbol can be understood only according to the inner experience of the actor. Although their concrete forms derive from the codified cultural orders, symbols are directly connected to the individual and collective imagination. As products of the Imaginary, symbols are a free elaboration of the cultural resources available in the historical and social context, and their specific meaning often does not correspond to the codified meanings of the prevailing symbolic-normative order. As a matter of fact, the meanings of individual life experience, which develop in the specific imaginary world of the individual experience from childhood onwards, are not necessarily the same as the collectively shared meanings (see Castoriadis, 1975).

Obviously, the sociological analysis of action will mainly take into account the codified forms of the prevailing symbolic-normative order orientating social behaviour as basic elements for the construction of social reality, but the possibility should not be overlooked that collective behaviours are orientated by the Imaginary, as different from or even opposed to the codified meanings. Youth or religious movements, terrorism, the infatuation for a charismatic leader and so on, show a predominance of the Imaginary that needs to be analysed into its proper components and meanings.

Between the two opposed ideal models – first, a behaviour entirely integrated in the prevailing symbolic-normative system, and secondly, a behaviour entirely orientated by imaginary meanings (as in the case of paranoia) – stand the concrete social behaviours related in many different ways to Symbolic, Imaginary and Reality.

The fact that any human action is also a *symbol* explains the complexities and difficulties of its interpretation: human action, even when it appears directly connected to the biological functions of survival, is never exhausted by the latter, but has a *sense* that, being partly related to the general cultural code, is also connected with the specific codes of the individual or of his particular group (ethnic, sexual, age, professional and so on).

If the individual as an *identity* is largely a product of the sociocultural context, the negative capacity of consciousness allows the individual, both consciously and unconsciously to establish from the beginning of his life some defences against the outer environment. Thus, as a result of his own biographical experience, the individual develops his own system of meanings through selective and repressive mechanisms. The set of private imaginary and symbolic meanings never entirely coincides with the shared social meanings. This means that each specific action of the individual cannot be interpreted only with reference to the objective natural or social function expressed by it, but must also be referred to the specific experience of the actor himself. Consequently, even the apparently most simple and natural actions, such as eating, have to be interpreted in relation to symbols, both *social* (meanings connected with social participation and solidarity, codes of honour, rituals and the rest) and *personal* (for example, the compensation function of food in its relation to frustration, aggression and so on).

The imaginary character of social action involves all the manifestations of the latter, and from this standpoint there is no distinction between practical or purposive actions and actions inspired either by aesthetical, political, ethical or religious values. In this aspect, the Aristotelian distinction between *poiesis* and *praxis* appears to be artificial, although, as we said before, it is useful for showing that not every action is reducible to the utilitarian model. The individual does not live his experience of the original emptiness or his need of meaning only at an intellectual level but also when he is working, when he has to solve an economic or technical problem or adapt to biological needs.

The symbolic dimension of action is as strong at the *poiesis* level as at the *praxis*: this explains why, even in formal organizations which should be orientated by the model of rational purposive action, there are so many 'non-rational' or 'irrational' behaviours, which can be understood only with reference to the specific imaginary world of the social actors and to the particular type of involvement with the objects they have sublimated. This confirms our previous critique of the utilitarian model and shows that action has to be interpreted within the 'inner coherence' of its actual meaning.

3.2 INSECURITY AND IDENTITY

The gap opened by the questioning about being-in-the-world and by the infinite character of desire explains why the situation of the individual in the world is generally characterized by ontologic insecurity, bewilderment, anguish and boredom.

First, the insecurity about our effective being is directly connected with the consciousness of being-in-the-world, as the latter is also awareness of the possibility of not being there, that is, of death. As Sartre remarked, the frailty of man is linked to the fact that 'his being involves as such the possibility of not being' (Sartre, 1943, p. 43). The consciousness of being can give way to a strong joyful feeling, such as Lacan evidenced in his analysis of the *'stade du miroir'* (Lacan, 1966, p. 93), as well as to feelings of anxiety and fear.

Secondly, the insecurity of the individual is connected with the uncertainty of having a social identity and being recognized and accepted by others. Acknowledgement by others is in fact an essential condition for reassurance about the effective consistency of our being. Bewilderment and anguish derive, on the one hand, from the feeling of not having a certain *ubi consistam* and, on the other, from the question about our future destiny in this or, eventually, in an after-death life: 'I am not what I will be' (Sartre, 1943, p. 69). This aspect stresses the temporal dimension (past, present, future) of life experience and social action that has been widely analysed by Alfred Schütz (1932).

Due to this essential insecurity the problem of *identity*, at both individual and collective levels, appears to be of the greatest relevance to the interpretation of social action. Any form of identity, precisely because it is *determined*, is reductive of the complexity of the individual being. Although the individual depends on it for reassurance about his actual being and for the possibility of establishing mutual relations with others, identity is also, in the final analysis, always perceived by him as a limitation.

The search for identity and consequent mutual recognition can well be considered as a general deep motivation grounding any individual and collective action (see Crespi, 1985, p. 377). In this case, too, the concrete forms through which confirmation of identity is sought can be very different from one another and the imaginary symbols can take part in the same process in many different ways.

The polyvalent character of the forms through which identity is constructed leads to further complexity because, in order to reach an identity recognized by others in both interpersonal and wider social world relations, the individual can sometimes be compelled to appeal to negative identifications. Just as in order to be 'seen' by adults, the child prefers to be punished rather than ignored, so many criminal or 'mad' behaviours can be explained by the need to obtain social recognition in one way or another.

As Mead has stressed, mutual recognition is also at the basis of the relation established by the individual with his own Self. We experience ourselves as worthy of recognition only if others have loved us and treated us as deserving such recognition (see Tugendhat, 1984). Self-contempt prevents one from establishing a positive relation with oneself and influences the relation of the individual to others just as the original experience of the attitude of others was the cause of self-esteem.

An aspect of the temporal dimension of the problem of identity is related to the conception of the ego, either as a sequence of successive different moments or as a stable unit. As is well known, the historical perception of personality has varied according to the different cultural contexts (see Carrithers et al., 1985). However, it seems that some constant components, related to desire, the need for identity, anxiety and death, can be defined beyond the different historical forms. Every culture attempts to answer these fundamental existential problems and to supply them with some form of expression.

The ambivalent relation with one's own identity appears to be a constant factor of the human situation as such: on the one hand, the individual seeks some form of objective identification, but on the other, despite the risks it implies, he tends to distance himself from the codified forms of identification. If the individual is too identified with the codified cultural representations and social roles he risks being taken for granted, and thus *not seen*, to the same extent as if he had no identity at all.

Even if it were true that in other sociocultural contexts individuality had not the same value as in our tradition, it is certainly true that every society has had to deal with the problem of controlling deviant behaviours. This proves that human beings have always had the capacity to differentiate themselves from the prevailing social order.

The fragmentation and changes that the individual experiences during his life notwithstanding, a certain unity of his personality seems to persist. As Ion Elster, a philosopher who is far from being a metaphysician, has remarked: 'we ought not to take the notion of "several selves" very literally. In general, we are dealing with exactly *one* person – neither more nor less. That person may have some cognitive problems of coordination, and some motivational conflicts, but it is *his* job to sort them out' (Elster, 1985, p. 30).

In recent years, sociological analysis has given increasing consideration to social actors' need to be reassured about their identities. Charles Taylor has stressed the difference between *strong* and *weak* values that orientate action. In *weak evaluations* 'for something to be judged good it is sufficient that it be desired', whereas in *strong evaluations* 'there is also a use of "good" or other evaluative terms for which being desired is not sufficient; indeed some desires or desired consummations can be judged as bad, base, ignoble, trivial, superficial, unworthy, and so on' (Taylor, 1985, p. 18).

The presence of *strong evaluations* shows that the dimensions of honour and prestige are very important for understanding social action, as the latter, beyond being driven by concrete interests, often appears to be orientated by the aspiration to be 'a certain kind of person' (Taylor, 1985, p. 19).

In the same direction, Alessandro Pizzorno has recently stressed the importance of the criteria of loyalty and social actors' need for identification and recognition to interpret social dynamics: 'an individual identifies himself with a group not for any specific purpose, but because he derives his own identity by identifying himself with the whole reality of the group' (Pizzorno, 1986). He also points out that the identity of the individual is strictly linked to the temporal dimension: this shows that a rational choice based on the forecast of its consequences is practically impossible. In fact, since in our societies social recognition is not always guaranteed by the same forms of organization but has to be sought in ever-new forms, the present interests of the actor's ego are not the same as those of his future ego. According to Pizzorno, 'the purpose of my actions is not to acquire utility, but to ensure recognition'.

It is in these terms that the contemporary theory of social action seems to be shifting from the rational to the phenomenological and hermeneutic model, from a utilitarian to an 'ontological' perspective. Rather than specific aims social action appears to be seeking *being*. In this case rationality is not reducible to the strategies for the fulfilment of the actor's material interests, but has to be interpreted with the more complex inner logic of an action orientated mainly to founding identity and mutual predictability through the changing requirements of life experience.

Among the many examples of how the problem of identity and prestige can influence action, even in situations which seem to require a maximum of responsibility and rationality as well as a high control of emotionality, a good one is that reported by Hough (1980) in his biography of Lord Mounbatten. Although Churchill had sent Mountbatten to South-East Asia to prepare a plan to defeat the Japanese, Mountbatten had the feeling that Churchill, afraid of losing his historical position as the unique saviour of the free world, had at the last moment cancelled the Buccaneer operation (against the Japanese), thus contradicting the instructions that he had given him only seven weeks before. We are not interested here in establishing if Mountbatten's interpretation of Churchill's behaviour was right, but in remarking that it is plausible, that similar interpretations could be given of a great number of behaviours precisely within those economic, political or scientific organizations which should only be inspired by functional models and purposive rationality (see Kernberg, 1980). In this kind of organization, too, action often involves subjective aspects connected with identity, honour or prestige, that is, with the symbolic character of objects and events in individual and collective desire and imagination. A theory of action which did not take into account such aspects would give a very inadequate interpretation of social dynamics.

3.3 ACTION AS INVOLVEMENT: CARE AND RESPONSIBILITY

As we have stressed more than once, from the beginning action is involved in a concrete situation: before any self-consciousness arises the social actor finds himself thrown among material and cultural conditions independent of his will.

The fact that the actor is originally caught in a situation not only explains why his identity is mainly determined by the society to which he belongs but also shows that he finds himself acting in a context where the meanings of things are predetermined by symbolic representations, uses, mores, techniques and so on.

The actor's involvement in his environment (*Umwelt*) has been characterized by Heidegger as *Umgang*, namely, to have-to-do-with-things, and *Sorge*, namely, to take care of things by their manipulation and use (see Heidegger, 1927, p. 80). Through the mediation of language and the example of others, the instrumental meanings of things are intuitively known by the individual, to the point that we can say that, before giving them any thought, the social actor is first introduced to the world of shared meanings by his instrumental relation with things.

Precisely because they appear as *tools*, as 'something for', things are part of an already socially qualified totality, which is somehow prior to any single object: 'Before the single tool, a totality of tools is already discovered' as the single tool has its meaning in the context of its use, or *Zuhandenheit* (see Heidegger, 1927, p. 82). In coming out from a totality of shared meanings, the practical dimension of use shows, on the one hand, that even the most 'material' action is connected with a complexity of meaning, while, on the other hand, it explains the pre-predicative dimension of action. The social actor finds himself already acting and only afterwards he becomes aware of his own actions and Self. This character of action is connected with different aspects, namely the *bodily* dimension in a world of other physical organisms, and the aforementioned *temporal* dimension.

Involvement in a system of action already connected with an organized and symbolically mediated world takes place not only through language and social representations but also with the different techniques of manipulation and use of things: this shows that the horizon of action and its consequences in the flow of time are never entirely under the control of the actors. The forms of action have a temporal continuity that cannot be interrupted by will: we find ourselves in a stream of actions whose present and future effects we don't entirely know. For this reason the theory of social action must also take into account the positive or negative *unwanted effects* of action (see Boudon, 1977).

At the social level, the irreversible and unpredictable character of action implies a certain anonymity as to the responsibility of action while, at the same time, it involves the actor in a sort of responsibility which is attributed to him *before* he can choose it. In this same perspective one should take into account Heidegger's analysis of the anonymity of *They* (they say, they think . . .) and of *chatter*, as well as the dimensions of alienation (Marx) and the otherdirectedness (Riesman) of action.

Thus, for an adequate orientation of the theory of action, beside the interpretation of action in its connection with desire and the imaginary and symbolic orders, it is also necessary to consider the relative autonomy of action, its impact on subjective intentionality which often determines the social actors' behaviour to the point that they can well be considered as the *product* of the concrete system of action.

On the basis of the presuppositions that I have tried to clarify there is, however, neither a pure creativity nor a pure passivity of the social actor. Self-reflexivity and the capacity to distance oneself from the objectified forms through negation, show that the actor is never merely a product of social structures. In this direction the concept of alienation should be reconsidered, for even actors who are better identified with their social roles never appear to be mere products of alienation but, rather, persons who, despite difficulties and coercions, are trying to save their lives and identities by means of an accentuated compliance with codified social rules. In this case, too, actors tend to elaborate their own experiences and meanings and somehow live *their own* life. The problem here is not to analyse the different degrees of freedom of the social actors but to stress the relativity of the concepts of alienation and passivity when applied to human beings.

Beside the instrumental dimension and the possibility of an autonomous development of action as such, we must also consider the *intersubjective* dimension as an aspect of the involving character of action. By intersubjectivity I mean the original being-with-others dimension of the existential situation that Heidegger stressed in terms of *Mit-sein* and *Mit-dasein*. Whereas Husserl conceives the I as originally isolated from and prior to any intersubjective relation, Heidegger's *being with* is a constitutive element of being-in-the-world (see Heidegger, 1927, p. 127). As with the instrumental relation with things, the inter-subjective relation is also prior to any consciousness and understanding: 'we greet the other before knowing him' (Levinas, 1972).

3.4 ACTION AND TRANSCENDENCE

The pre-predicative responsibility towards the other shows a level of experience which is somehow 'more than social'. Our relation with the other has a deeper ground than the symbolic-normative order of communication: to recognize the other as *other* implies not merely the taken-for-granted identification of his social role but the acknowledgement of his *difference*, that is, the unfathomable dimension which characterizes him as an ego. Just as in our relations with ourselves we look for identifications with others while at the same time trying to differentiate ourselves from them, so in our relations with the other we tend initially to refer him to the experience of ourselves, but subsequently we must recognize his diversity.

In this context, the responsibility towards the other appears to be not only a relation grounded on *justice*, the result of a utilitarian calculus, but also an *ethical* relation implying deeper links irreducible to the advantages of reciprocity and social control.

Apart from his need for social identity, the social actor also develops an intrinsic refusal of social determinations, thus showing an un-social dimension which explains why a total integration of the individual into the social system is impossible. This aspect was called by Kant the 'un-social sociability' of the human being, that is, 'the tendency to join society, connected with a general aversion to be totally integrated in society itself' (Kant, 1913). However, Kant ascribes un-sociability only to the psychological selfishness of the individual, while from the perspective I have tried to develop in these pages, unsociability also appears to be connected with the ontological dimension as total integration in the social system would entail the end of the individual as such.

The different aspects of infinite desire, pre-predicative responsibility and limited integration justify the use of the term *transcendence* with relation to action: this term is actually another way of showing that action has deeper roots than the normative-functional level of the social system. The transcendence of action shows the *tragic* dimension of the latter, if by tragic we refer to the impossibility of conciliation (Hegel), to a conflict without resolution (Goethe), or to a contradiction that cannot be overcome (Kierkegaard).

As we mentioned previously, the dimension of desire shows a radical lack of fulfilment, while the oscillation of the social actors between the need for identity and predictability and the opposed need for distantiation and difference appears to be an insuperable contradiction. Action is thus strictly connected with the irreconcilable character of the social situation as such, which is due to the indeterminacy of the negative dimension of consciousness. Negative dimension-indeterminacy-transcendency allow us to understand Kant's concept of freedom as 'unconditional causality'. Precisely because freedom, or the 'I' as the active principle at its origin, reveals itself only as the capacity to negate the objectivated forms, we cannot grasp it directly but only as the specific indeterminacy of the transcendence of action as opposed to the definite forms of social order.

The unconditional dimension of action always escapes empirical analysis because, once accomplished, any free choice is already symbolically mediated, that is, determinate and historically conditioned. Therefore freedom can be understood only as the *shifting* from one form of determinacy to another, but this quick passage cannot be directly perceived. This is why, as we shall see later (Chapter Five), we can empirically analyse the *traces* of action as *signs* of a more complex reality.

The explanation of the real processes of action has its limits in the unconditional character of freedom, which remains unknown as such. This is why scientific analysis is always tempted to overlook indeterminacy by merely describing determinacy. But when this analysis loses the perception of its own limits, then it also loses sight of that oscillation between *identification with* and *distantiation from* determinacy which is essential to action. The theory of action has a paradoxical character that must be maintained as such, for its final 'in-conclusiveness', when duly recognized, allows maximum understanding of action's depth and complexity.

If my argument has some basis, then all the aspects of action considered here lead us to the analysis of another crucial concept for the theory of action: *power*. Power, in fact, appears to be a dimension directly connected to dealing with the inner contradictions as well as to the specific decision-making processes of action.

4

Power

> 'Talleyrand was shamelessly disregarding the same principle of legitimacy that he had asserted as the ground of his action.'
>
> R. Calasso

Power, in the sense I am using it here, appears as the moment when the impossibility of reducing action to symbolic-normative order and the 'tragic' character of action are clearly revealed.

Power, as we shall see, is mainly decision, choice, capacity to deal with the unavoidable contradictions of the relation between action and norms. Decision-making is an act that can be interpreted neither as a merely cognitive phenomenon nor as a pure compliance with rules. A decision is often made in a situation where one is 'at a loss' in dealing with contingencies for which there are no clear orientations or patterns of behaviour.

Precisely because power is connected with the *practical* dimension of action, as having-to-do-with-things, intuition and the management of contradictions, and also because power allows one to analyse concrete social relations within the structures of social inequality, I consider power to be sociologically more meaningful than the term *phronesis*.

The concept of *phronesis* in the Aristotelian tradition refers to the prudential capacity to mediate practical activities which cannot be submitted to such clear and coercive rules as those of *poiesis*. *Phronesis* can be conceived of as a *habitus*, a virtue acquired through practical experience allowing one to judge contingent situations without emotionality and without being influenced by appearances: a capacity to evaluate relatively free from preconceived models. At the cognitive level, *phronesis* allows one to determine 'which between two solutions to a theoretical dilemma offers the best possible arrangement of accuracy, validity, simplicity, coherence and fecundity' (Ferrara, 1986).

Compared to the concept of *phronesis*, which refers mainly to epistemological and ethical dimensions, the concept of *power*, in the sense I use it here, although it has some analogies with *phronesis*, appears to be more complex. It refers not only to individual qualities of judgement but also to social action as such with all its ambivalence. Whereas *phronesis* always has a positive meaning, *power* includes both positive and negative aspects, showing the contradictions of action and the irreconcilable character of social situations. On the one hand, power appears as the capacity to deal with those contradictions, and on the other, it appears as a 'minor evil', as a function and structure related to the impossibility of a final solution of the social problem.

In the following pages we shall consider these aspects further, but here I want to stress that the concept of power leads us from an abstract to a concrete analysis of action. Even if we still have to consider the general theoretical elements of power, we should take into account that it is only possible to develop a specific sociological analysis of social dynamics with reference to power. Many studies in the social field tend to consider exclusively the cultural or psychological aspects of the construction of social reality, but it is when power dynamics are analysed that the *focus* of the sociological approach is actually revealed.

4.1 SOCIALITY AND NORMATIVE ORDER

The structures of the social system have their roots in the intersubjective relations which involve social actors in reciprocal responsibility and in the pre-predicative relation with things and tools. Both these relations are interconnected, as the relation with things develops only in a context of intersubjectively shared meanings, while the relations between individuals are always constituted within a material structure of bodies and things. Obviously, both relations develop only through the mediation of symbolic orders of social representations (language, symbols, values) and norms.

Social structures are relatively coherent systems of symbolic-normative forms which define the difference between individuals (sex, age, physical characters, functions, roles and the rest), establish the relations between individuals and things (resources, property), orientates technical procedures, sets collective goals and so on.

The necessary *and* reductive character of such systems of mediation is at the origin of the tension deriving from the ambivalent relation between action and forms of mediation, at both the individual level of identity and the social level in which we find the opposed requirements of predictability and adaptation to change. As we shall see more clearly later (section 4.4), the same reductive character of social forms of mediation is also at the origin of social inequality and conflict.

The analysis of the genesis of social structures shows a continuity between the different institutional forms and the action producing them. Subsequently social structures, as objectivated products of action, acquire autonomy and in turn become conditions for the production of social actors and action. At this point, the fact that action originated structures tends to be forgotten.

The general categories that I have applied to action are also useful for the analysis of the phenomenology of power, as the most important momentum of praxis and the intersecting point between action and structures. The relation between consciousness and symbolic mediation and the oscillation between the opposing needs for *identification with* objectivated forms (such as identity, social predictability, cognitive certainty, collective representations) and *distantiation from* determinacy (difference between the 'I' and social identity, desire and Imaginary, adaptation to change, and so on) are at the basis of my definition of power.

The social order is essentially based on shared meanings and values, as well as on norms which provide the necessary reciprocal predictability of action. In order to survive every society must have a 'code' which is the conventional result of intersubjective experience in its relation to the material and cultural conditions of the concrete situation. The code, or system of symbolic-normative forms of mediation, can be diffused by oral tradition, it can find expression in mores or be written in formal laws, and its rules can be explicit or implicit, manifest or latent. All these different aspects are usually present at the same time in our societies.

As I have stressed above, reflexivity and the reductive character of the symbolic forms create problems in human society: unlike animal societies where the behaviour of the individual is strictly determined by instinctual mechanisms, human society consists of self-conscious individuals having the capacity to differentiate themselves from forms of determinacy which constitute social reality, and even from their own social identity. If it is true that culture shapes social actors from birth, it is also true that, despite absolutization to the point of appearing like *nature*, culture never succeeds in regulating human action with a determinism as consistent as natural instincts. No cultural systems ever succeed in comprehending all the different issues of human experience. It is mainly for these reasons that human societies are much more susceptible to change and unpredictability than animal societies.

As we shall see later (section 4.2), social actors are never totally dependent on the socialization process but, through their own experience, they can shape relatively autonomous meanings and personal codes. On the one hand, not being strictly linked to the cultural forms that determine his own social identity, the individual can oppose the social order and give way to a sort of *hubris*, considering himself an absolute entity free from any duty and authority. On the other hand, beside his potential anarchic dimension, the social actor cannot do without a determined identity which can only be constituted within an intersubjectively shared realm of meanings: there is no identity without reciprocal recognition.

There is no way to avoid the oscillation between determinacy and indeterminacy specific to the aforementioned 'unsocial sociability' of the actor: while pure unsociability would drive the actor to a total lack of communication with others and loss of his own Self, a total integration in the social system would reduce him to a merely social role, again depriving him of his inner identity. The only possibility open to the actor is to maintain an unstable equilibrium between these opposed needs.

The phenomenological analysis of the constitutive dimensions of the social situation thus shows the essential ambivalence of social action in its relation with the *determinacy* of the symbolic-normative order and the *indeterminacy* due to the complexity of actual life experience. The faculty which qualifies the social subjects, either individual or collective, as capable of dealing with this contradictory situation is what I call here *power*. In this context the function of power appears to be consequent on the impossibility of considering the social reality only as normative order and the need to analyse that reality in terms of the dynamic relation between action and the normative–institutional dimension. Society does not function only through the observance of norms: the rigid observance of norms kills a social system, as it is shown by the concept of 'functional inobservance' (see Manciulli et al., 1986), and the possibility of protest in every social organization through the literal application of written rules ('work by the book' or *'grèves du zèle'*). Social systems also function through continual infringements of norms, in a process of constant adaptation between the requirements of practical action and the need to maintain predictability and social order.

In this perspective a general definition of power can be given in the following terms: *power is the function which allows the specific contradictions of the relation between determinacy and indeterminacy to be dealt with*. This function can be analysed at two levels: (a) the *subjective*, both as an *inner* capacity of the individual in his relation with his own determinations (Self, identity) and with the conditions of his concrete social situation, and as an *outer*, or attributed from outside, capacity to deal with the contradictions of social reality; and (b) the *objective*, or *structural* level, where the function of dealing with the contradictions between determinacy and indeterminacy appears to be a specific mechanism of the normative-institutional order itself.

Each of the three different dimensions of power (inner subjective, outer subjective, objective) can be related to a specific analytical context: the first dimension is mainly connected with the existential experience of the individual and is mainly analysed by *psychology*; the second refers to the sphere of social intersubjectivity and symbolic interaction and is mainly analysed by *social psychology*; the third refers mainly to structural and normative aspects and to the action-structure relation, and has to do with the *sociological* analysis of complex systems, as well as with juridical and politological approaches.

Although the term power implies specific meanings for each different level – *inner capacity*, attributed *social function*, *structure* – it is important not to lose sight of the fact that all these forms of power are linked to the essential problem of managing the contradictions of social action. As we shall see later, the possibility of establishing a relation among these different forms shows the limitations of outer power, the relevance and ambivalence of the structural dimension and finally the importance of strengthening the inner power of individuals. The lack of perception of the interconnections among the different aspects of power is one of the main causes of the inadequacy of contemporary theories of power.

In these theories power is generally understood as the capacity to produce effects. This is a too-generic definition of power. When, for example, we say that a group of terrorists has power, we generically refer to the capacity of that group to produce some threatening effects in social life. But in order to establish if the terrorist group has a chance to become new leaders of society we must apply the aforementioned categories of outer and structural power in terms of the capacity of the group to deal with the contradictions of the actual social situation. In this context the structures of the social system, the forms of symbolic-normative mediation leading to legitimation of power, the degree of inner power of the social actors as well as the material conditions, must be taken into account.

The same more-specific definition of power must also be applied when we want to analyse the dimension of power *within* the terrorist group. The leader (or leaders) of it will have to correspond to the requirements of the balance between determinacy and indeterminacy.

To better clarify the categories implied in this perspective I shall consider each different dimension of power separately.

4.2 INNER POWER

At birth the human individual has no power: the *in-fans* (the non-speaking child) is totally dependent on adults for survival, and even his capacity for self-recognition derives from adults' prior recognition of his being there. The individual's construction of identity and the modalities of his own experience of things and others are mediated by the symbolic forms available in the social community to which he belongs.

Since the earliest moments of life the individual undergoes an intensive socialization process which operates through cultural forms establishing the different aspects of life: food, clothing, relations with parents and other relatives, perceptions of environment and so on. It is well known that these cultural forms can vary widely according to different types of society, leaving a deep imprint on the social actors and determining their sensibility, their emotions, their representations of the world as well as of society (see Parsons, 1968; Gerth and Wright-Mills, 1953).

However, the process of interiorization of values and patterns of behaviour does not develop in a purely passive way. From the beginning there is an active element in the individual which, as part of his genetic set, orientates him to learning and psychological development (see Piaget, 1979). The reflexive dimension of consciousness acts as the capacity to select among different experiences and to elaborate them through memory. As Melanie Klein's analyses have pointed out (Klein, 1952), the child is capable from a very early age of establishing defensive strategies which in the end produce structures that reinforce as well as more or less limit his personality. Qualifying the life experience of each individual, these defences are rooted in the capacity to negate the objectivated forms which, as we have already seen, is an essential feature of consciousness. Thanks to the capacity to accumulate experiences, which is connected with the temporal continuity of consciousness, the individual can select and build up a personal system of meanings and symbols, only partly corresponding to the prevailing cultural order.

The individual, both at the conscious and unconscious level, progressively speaks to himself in a sort of 'private language' which functions as a 'filter' of the different stimuli coming from the outside world. Obviously, I am talking only loosely of a 'private language' which, as Wittgenstein pointed out, is impossible as such (see Bouveresse, 1976). I am merely referring here to the personal 'translation' of codes, whose origin is always intersubjective.

Once interiorized, the sociocultural codes are used by the individual as tools for expression and communication, but the meaning he perceives, though it is mediated by the same codes, does not necessarily coincide with the conventional meanings taken for granted in the everyday social world (see Schütz, 1932). Between the *inner world* of the individual, structured both by assimilation of the symbolic resources available in the social context and by personal elaboration of the same resources, and the *outer world* of the relations he establishes with things and others, there is thus a certain gap which allows the individual to lead a social life without giving up his own *difference*.

As already mentioned, the individual identity has, in fact, a characteristic ambivalence. On the one hand, in order to be accepted by others, one must be *similar* to them to a certain extent. On the other hand, in order to avoid anonymity and taken-for-grantedness, one must be *different* from others to a certain extent. The aforementioned oscillation of consciousness between *determinacy* (in this case, identity as similarity) and *indeterminacy* (identity as difference) also characterizes the relation of the individual with his own Self. It is evident here that the inner capacity for elaborating a personal meaning is as important to the individual's life as is his capacity for sharing social values and patterns of behaviour. The relative autonomy of his own inner identity, when compared to his outer social identity, allows him to use the latter as a *mask* which in no way expresses his entire personal identity: he can thus *distance* himself from the role society attributes him. With this device the individual normally protects himself from the danger of being totally alienated due to excessive identification with his social function (see Goffman, 1961, p. 137).

Consequently, one can say that an individual has *inner power* inasmuch as he is successful in dealing with the opposing requirements, on the one hand, of being socially determined in order to be accepted by others and, on the other hand, of maintaining his autonomy in order to avoid being flattened to his social image. Independence can, in fact, be obtained only by running the risk of questioning our socially codified identity and by refusing a total subordination to the same social system which grants us the essential resources for survival. To give a simple example, it is well known that somebody who cannot threaten to resign from his job can easily be reduced to slavery, while somebody who is unable to assume a definite 'role' in society can easily be reduced to a drop-out.

The Freudian analysis of the relation between ego and superego presents many connections with our concept of the individual's inner power. According to Freud, the ideal ego develops in the individual due to the critique his parents and other adults expressed verbally (see Freud, 1914, 1917). As is well known, in Freud the superego thus performs an essential function for building up the ego in its relation to the id: the superego in fact allows one to abandon the polymorphous infantile state and assures the strengthening of a coherent ego unity through progressive repressions and differentiations. But it is also true that in Freud the excessive dependence on the superego is considered an obstacle to the ego's real development. Freud recognizes the positive nature of the different conflicting identifications of the ego and, even more importantly from our point of view, he also positively considers the fact that after strengthening its identity, the ego can resist influences deriving from identification with the superego (see Freud, 1922).

While the development of the ego initially consists in distancing oneself from primary narcissism and driving the libido towards the ideal ego, subsequently it appears to be directly connected with release from domination by the ideal ego. This process develops either by achieving the ideal or by relativizing it through a reformulation which permits new possibilities (see Freud, 1921; Ferenczi, 1939; Adorno 1966; Ricoeur, 1965).

As we mentioned above (Chapter Two, section 2.7), George Mead also stressed the fact that the individual builds up his own identity only when he learns to consider himself through the image others send back to him, or rather, through the 'generalised Other' that summarizes the socially shared expectations: in other words, when the individual manages to consider himself as 'me'. But at the same time Mead shows that the individual develops fully only when, beyond the social image of 'me', he gets to that process of transcending 'me' which is specific to 'I'. According to Mead, the 'I' is always something different from what is required by the situation: the 'I' is the active and creative response to the codified attitudes of 'me' (Mead, 1934, pp. 218, 326).

The vital dynamic between ego and superego, 'I' and 'me', shows that the inner power of the actor is the capacity to deal with the contradictions of the individual's relation with his own Self, as well as with the determined forms of his social and natural environment. Inner power thus appears as the capacity for using the objectivated forms without considering them absolute, that is, recognizing both their necessity and their reductive character. This recognition implies taking risks: on the one hand, the individual must avoid falling into an excessive identification, or being reified and alienated in the object; on the other hand, he runs the risk of losing his identity, vanishing into indeterminacy and no longer being able to establish concrete relations with things and others.

The individual develops his inner power only when he faces both risks and is not afraid either of being involved in forms of identification or of dealing with the inner and outer dimensions of unpredictability and the unknown. Accepting his ontological insecurity (to be or not to be) and the irreconcilable character of the existential situation, the individual succeeds in establishing positive relations with the 'Imaginary' as well as with the symbolic order and 'reality'. In his deep identity he can thus integrate different meanings deriving from both past and present experiences and he can open up to the future. As post-Freudian psychoanalytic theory has pointed out, the strength of the ego is grounded in the capacity to 'keep together' a coherent Self rather than in a stable 'essence' of the ego (see Kohut, 1969; Winnicott, 1965). The more the individual succeeds in this complex operation, the more he can become a source of reassurance for others, promoting their autonomy: inner power develops then as wisdom, love, practical capacity, responsibility and so on.

Inner power as such is not connected with a will to dominate others: on the contrary, the more inner power an individual has, the less he needs to look for reassurance by possessing or controlling others. Inner power strengthens in the individual his awareness of being: it frees him from the search for illusory reassurance in the absolutization of objectivated forms (dogmatic truth, role, ideologies and the rest) and leads him to recognize the radical impossibility of fulfilling his desire. Thus the individual who has developed inner power cannot only affirm his relative autonomy from others but also recognize his relative dependence on them, that is, the fact of being involved from the beginning in the intersubjective relation.

Obviously, I am referring here to the ideal type of individual who has an entirely developed inner power. We shall have to distinguish different degrees of inner power along a continuum starting from the total dependence of the *in-fans* and ending in the maximum degree of autonomy. However, it is not possible to measure directly the effective level of inner power reached by a person: precisely because it is the result of an inner achievement, this kind of power need not show. The more an individual has inner power, the less he tries to get from others an outer power, and if he has to exercise the latter he does it more from a sense of duty than from choice.

4.3 OUTER POWER

We must now consider the second aspect of subjective power: that which develops in the intersubjective social relations of members of a concrete society. Whereas in the case previously analysed the term 'individual' was used in its literal meaning, when we refer to *outer power* the subject can be either a single man or woman or a group of people.

Outer power, as well as inner power, is the capacity to deal with the specific contradictions of the relation between determinacy and indeterminacy, but in this case the term power no longer refers to the individual's inner world but rather to external social relations in their connection with material conditions and institutional structures. At this level, power appears to be strictly related to the function of complexity reduction which is at the basis of the maintenance of social order, namely, the function ensuring the essential conditions for adaptation of the normative social systemic structures to the changing requirements of life experience, action and environment.

It is at this analytical level that the link between action and power shows itself most clearly: power appears to be the consequence of the aforementioned fact that action is irreducible to normative order. Power is the function ensuring the necessary balance between the objectivated forms of symbolic mediation, always reductive of the complexity of life experience, and the changing needs of social action.

As I have already pointed out, in order to maintain the social order it is necessary to base the reciprocal predictability of social actions on stable and determinate symbolic mediation forms. Its achievement requires a *legislator* capable of translating into synthetic norms the complex needs of social life and, once the norms are formulated, it requires a *judge* capable of interpreting and applying them to concrete situations in order to guarantee the effective compliance with norms, sometimes even by coercion. In order to make norms effective it is in fact necessary to balance the need for determinacy which founds predictability (certainty of law) with the need for adaptation to the specific conditions of the situation (interpretation of the norm with equity and justice), but it is also necessary that some means of control and imposition be available (function of police).

However, as we have already seen, social life is not merely an application of norms nor a system of sanctions: it is also life experience, reaction to events, decision and project. All these dimensions are susceptible of becoming opposed to the established norms and can provoke new situations for which no norms have been foreseen. Hence the need of an executive or *political* function separate from the legislative and judiciary ones.

All these functions are forms of outer power. We can analytically distinguish other concrete forms as well: ideological, economic, military and so on (see Mann, 1986, p. 22). In order to show the general aspects of outer power I shall consider here only the specific political-executive function and disregard other distinctions or connections. I believe, in fact, that the basic components of political power can be applied to any other particular form of outer power. If judiciary power already implies a decisional dimension in the exercise of equity, political power eminently appears as the function that ensures the necessary adjustments in contingent situations will be made through decision-making processes, without putting into question the legal order or creating unbearable degrees of unpredictability.

The political function of decision in the social system has a certain analogy with the function of the ego in the personal system: in fact, the executive function has not only to deal with those 'macro' equivalents of the drives that are the collective movements but it also has to reduce the pretences of the normative order (which plays here the role of ideal ego). It thus appears that the function of *representation* of the different components of society specific to political power should not be emphasized (as the Left tends to do) to the detriment of the *decisional* function (emphasized by the Right): in this case too, the relation between the two functions has to be dealt with in its unavoidable contradictory aspects which are consequent on the ambivalent character of social action.

The function of political power is essentially based on its real or alleged capacity to frame laws and to guarantee their observance and, at the same time, to modify or even infringe established rules by filling eventual normative voids with decisions or by correcting normative forms which have become inadequate to actual social conditions. Thus, political power appears as a function that not only meets the need for predictability, but also responds to the vital need to oppose the tendency to reify normative forms. Power in this case is not *above* the law but develops dialectic relations with it, both as guarantor and as transgressor of the normative order. Without the dimension of power the mediating function of the symbolic forms (which, being determined, always tend to become absolute) would be smothered by the fatal process of crystallization which, sooner or later, endangers the relation with life experience which is essential for the effectiveness of the same mediating function.

It is with respect to this circumstance that a certain 'cynicism' appears to be an integral, although alarming, part of the function of power: the image of Talleyrand affirming the principle of legitimacy while disregarding it in his actions (see Calasso, 1983, p. 79) corresponds to a universal characteristic of the exercise of power.

As a social function, political power can be characterized as *outer* in that it does not necessarily correspond to the inner qualities of an individual but is, rather, the result of *attributing* to one or more individuals the capacity to deal with the contradictory relation between determinacy and indeterminacy. The attribution may rest on very different foundations, both from the point of view of the qualities of the leader whose power is being recognized (strength, beauty, intelligence, skills and so on) and from that of the motivations of the social actors attributing power (such as faith in his charisma, interest, fear).

The attribution of power by others puts the leader in a position where, up to a certain point, he can affirm values and norms *for others* without being himself totally dependent on them. It is precisely on this 'duplicity' that the discretionary nature of power is based; that is, the possibility of modifying or even infringing some of the rules without necessarily putting the whole normative order and its legitimation into crisis. Thus, the continuity of social order is maintained despite a constant change of content.

The ambiguity or duplicity of power, as legislator *and* transgressor of the norms, as a source of reassurance *and* of alarm, is specific to the function of outer power and in this regard it must be considered positive. A political power that is too dependent on prevailing values or ideological commitment, as well as on the literal observance of laws, generally lacks that capacity of adaptation to actual historical conditions which is essential to guarantee effective decisions and creative innovations when facing unpredictable events.

From a merely practical point of view, the ideal type of individual holding outer power is that of a leader who, although he has doubts, can give certainties to others or who, although he favours change, can maintain a certain continuity in the social order. Thus the capacity of simulating and dissimulating of the Macchiavellian prince should not always be considered as evil, even if it exemplifies the disquieting character of power as such.

Outer power in fact can be, on the one hand, reassuring for it relieves the pressure of collective responsibilities, but, on the other hand, it always implies the possibility of an overbearing imposition. Power can always degenerate into a form of totalitarianism, thus breaking the delicate balance between the opposed tendencies of the determinacy–indeterminacy relation. As we shall see later (section 4.5), power tends either to absolutize the forms of its own legitimation, thereby losing its creative capacity of decision-making by becoming too dependent on the normative order, or to turn into a purely arbitrary form of dominance, thereby giving way to an excessive degree of indeterminacy which will finally undermine the foundations of its own legitimation.

In the attribution of power two main elements can be distinguished: the first is *objective* and appears to be connected with the specific requirements of complexity reduction on which every social order is grounded (see Luhmann, 1975). The second is *subjective* and must be referred to the tendency to put the burden of the responsibilities, which both inner and outer power imply, on to the leader.

Rather than by the lust for power, social actors are often driven by the unconscious or conscious desire to obey, thereby escaping risks and responsibilities. As is well known, the image of the leader readily becomes for the masses a privileged object of identification and reassurance.

The objective dimension of complexity reduction is connected with the collective need to maintain basic rules which allow all the various social games to be played. With respect to this general interest, the conflicts related to particular interests tend to be considered as secondary except in the case of revolutions. In this perspective it is difficult to distinguish between *consensus* and *coercion*, both of which coexist within the relation of power: consensus can often be the product of a subtle manipulation by power, while sometimes what appears to be coercion is merely the result of violence.

To the extent that the attribution comes from a social relation, outer power is always the product of an implicit or explicit *negotiation* between the one (or the few) who exercise power and those who are willing to comply with it for one reason or another.

However, when speaking of consensus and negotiation we have to take into account the various social positions of the social actors: it is not always, nor always in the same measure, that the delegation of power given by the different members of a society is due to free choice; on the contrary, very often it is due to some form of coercion. The 'delegation of responsibility' has many different aspects: the outer power of the leader does not rely entirely on the refusal of responsibility by other social actors, and even if the need of the social actors to be reassured about their own identity plays a relevant part in reinforcing power, we must not forget that compliance with power is also due to objective structural conditions (see section 4.4).

I am trying to show here the *factual* elements which are at the origin of the phenomenon of power; I am not developing a theory of power legitimation: this has necessarily to be related to the *ideal* requirements grounding 'legitimate' power. For our discourse it is sufficient to recognize the coexistence of consensus and coercion in outer power relations, while stressing the difficulty of distinguishing the two dimensions which are equally constitutive of those same relations.

Coercion or the possibility of imposing commands by physical force (see Weber, 1922) is essential to outer power inasmuch as it has to guarantee the functioning of the normative order and the political and social institutions even in situations of conflict between the interests of the institutions and those of the social actors, or even when the latter fight among themselves and threaten the survival of the social system. In other words, it is precisely the possibility of control through coercion which makes outer power a solid foundation of social predictability. The function of guarantor of norms, the discretional and arbitration function of power, could not exist without at least a minimal possibility of coercion. However, pure coercion is not sufficient for establishing a social relation: the actual threat of a gun has a paralysing effect on both the holder of the gun and the person who is threatened by it. In this case the relation cannot be articulated. If a social system somehow *functions* it means that in it there is at least a minimum of consensus. In any case, as Luhmann has stressed, the less power has to use coercion, the stronger it is (see Luhmann, 1975).

The coercion dimension of outer power is actually the reflection of the aforementioned absolutized character of the determined forms of symbolic mediation: as the result of the reduction of life experience complexity, any form of determination always has a *violent* character.

The unavoidable dimension of coercion in outer power shows the limitations of those theories of power which, as in functionalism, tend to consider it merely as an instrument for attaining common goals or as a generalized means for defining collective aims in order to mobilize mass energies. In this context power appears to be merely the result of consensus and legitimation. This approach undervalues the specific repressive element of the structural character of power (see section 4.4). Normally outer power has then to be considered *both* in its coercive and consensual aspects, along a continuum running between a maximum of the representative character of power and a minimum of coercion on one side, and a maximum of coercion and a minimum of representative character on the other.

In this same perspective the question whether to consider power a limited facility (the 'zero sum' argument) or a collective capacity susceptible of increase (see Parsons, 1957) should be analysed. Also in this case the two aspects are not, as many theories of power seem to believe, mutually exclusive: it all depends, in fact, on the conditions on which power is grounded and on the ways in which power is exercised. It is evident that the 'zero sum' rule does not apply to inner power, since the increase of an individual's inner power is to the advantage of others, while for outer power all will depend on its concrete forms. If the latter always implies, at least to a certain degree, a monopolization of control, it is also true that outer power can either be exercised to maintain the members of society in their dependence on power interests, thus giving way to an effective subtraction of power; or, in the ideal situation of a political power exercised for the people's advantage, it can enhance the inner and outer power of all members of society by increasing resources for the individuals' education as well as their chances of participating in the decision-making processes. The concrete forms of representation and mediation of individual and collective interests have a decisive influence on this aspect.

As I have already said, the present analysis only considers the factual conditions of outer power without asking what is the best possible form of power. If a concrete political power survives it means that, at least up to a certain degree and at a more or less high cost, it corresponds to the task of managing the contradictions of the particular social situation. It also means that in the same concrete situation there actually are no other leaders better able to exercise power. Despite being merely tautological, this statement shows why a power inspired by less-high ideals can be sometimes more efficient and, in the final analysis, less destructive than that inspired by higher but more Utopian values. Here, too, all depends on the actual capacity for applying the function of complexity reduction and for maintaining the balance between, on one side, the need of identity, predictability and order, and, on the other, the need for adaptation and change. Obviously, this doesn't mean that the prevailing power is always the best possible one in the given situation but that the question of a power that would function at less social cost, with more justice and in a better perspective of collective emancipation, should be considered first with reference to the ability to deal effectively with the contradictions of the social situation which political power, in its own ambivalence, is bound to exercise. On the practical level, success is for power a necessary, even if not a sufficient, condition.

4.4 STRUCTURAL POWER AND THE PRODUCTION OF INEQUALITY

So far I have considered the two aspects of power which are directly connected with subjectivity, in both its inner and outer dimensions. We must now analyse the *objective* or *structural* dimension of power. While there is a clear distinction between inner and structural power (even if there can be mutual influences between them, connected with the relevance of sociocultural factors for the constitution of individual identity, or with the possibility that subjective elements may transform social structures), it is more difficult to distinguish between outer and structural power. Only exceptionally is the attribution of power directed merely to the personality of the leader. More often it is the result of the relation between the subjective qualities of the leader and structural conditions.

While at the *subjective level* power can be considered either as an inner or an external capacity for dealing with the contradictions of the determinacy–indeterminacy relation, or as the result of the different attitudes of social actors towards the risks implied in the responsibilities of power, at the *objective* or *structural level* power appears instead to be a controlling device within the social system. In this case power is the objective result of social action and is inscribed in the various normative-institutional orders of society itself. At this level power appears mainly to be a *position* or a *status-role* in the social organization, which determines the behaviour of the leader (or leaders), limiting his competence and regulating power reproduction. In any case, this dimension of power can also be included in the general definition of power that I have given.

As a determinate system of symbolic-normative forms of mediation, every social institution establishes the requisites for becoming a leader and the ways in which power should be exercised: it also fixes beforehand the conditions of mutual predictability and adaptability that are in principle necessary for its survival in relation to the environment and other social institutions. The specific function of power in the institutionalized system can be thus interpreted as the codified transposition in the symbolic-normative order of the relation between action and the objectivated mediation forms. In order not to lose their characteristic of mediation of practical experience, the symbolic-normative forms must avoid crystallization. This explains why through power the institutional order has to provide a device ensuring flexibility and limiting the pretences to absolutization of the normative order.

The capacity to deal with the contradictions of the determinacy–indeterminacy relation, which I have considered first as an inner or outer quality of the individual, now appears to be objectivated in the forms of symbolic-normative mediation. Translating Weber's historical distinction into an analytical one, one could say that the 'exceptional' character of individual power changes into the 'everyday life' form of structural power. For this reason the concept of power as structure is also the connecting point between the theory of social action and the theory of social system (see section 4.5). Whether we consider it from a subjective or structural point of view, power appears to be the meeting point of symbolic order and action, as the moment when both the symbolic order and life experience have, as it were, to recognize their mutual debt: on the one hand, the symbolic-normative mediation has to recognize its limits in the face of the transcendent and tragic character of action, while the latter has to recognize the stability and continuity afforded by the determined forms of mediation.

The analysis of the structural dimension of power, however, should not be limited to the phenomenon of the transposition of the function of power in the codified normative order, but should also consider that the power structure is the result of social action in its relation to material and social system conditions. In this perspective the power structure can be analysed in terms of *inequality* and *class*.

According to the presuppositions that I have so far tried to point out, inequality does not appear to be connected only to the 'natural' qualities of the different social actors, nor even only to the distortions produced by intentional or unintentional effects of social action, but it also seems to be a consequence of the reductive character of the forms of symbolic mediation as such. Even when trying to develop universal principles (language, world's representations, rights of man and so on), symbolic determination, in its normative character, cannot avoid being the product of the selection of *some* of the possibilities of action with the denial of all others (see Luhmann, 1971).

As we saw earlier, since the identity of individuals is constituted by the determined forms of the symbolic system, in the early stages of their life social actors can make their life experiences only through the mediation of that same system. But the *personal* identity of the individual never totally coincides with his *social* identity: in their particular situation individuals can develop, in a more or less active or reactive way, other forms of mediation, building up a personal identity different from the one attributed to them by the prevailing symbolic system.

In connection with the specific experience of each individual or each social group or subgroup, a differentiation develops which is due not only to the distribution of status role by the dominant social order, but also to the different degree of correspondence between that order and the actual experience of the social actors. With reference to the changes offered by the social system, specific positions of centrality or marginality are thus established, giving way to cultural subsystems (connected with groups, classes, ethnicity and the rest) which can be different from or even opposed to the prevailing symbolic-normative order and which may in turn sometimes become dominant systems.

The origin of inequality should then be related also to the reductive character of the symbolic-normative determinations, which can never exhaust the different requirements of the social actors. If individuals perfectly coincided with their social identities there would be no inequality problem, for each individual would be entirely realized, as in animal society, in the performance of his role in the social organization. But since individuals find themselves trapped from the beginning in contradictions deriving from self-consciousness, they suffer for the varying degree of correspondence between the chances that are offered them by the general symbolic-normative system and their particular expectations which are the result of a specific elaboration of meanings and values.

At the subjective level the inequality of social positions can be connected with the different degrees of individual inner and outer power, while at the structural level it appears to be a consequence of the reductive character of the determined symbolic forms as well as of the different distribution of resources.

The relation between power and class structure should also be analysed from the same perspective. I shall not expound on this aspect here, but let me just remind you that the reference to the connection between inequality and the reductive character of the symbolic-normative forms of mediation may lead us to redefine the concept of class which, beside the structure of work organization and property, also includes differences deriving from central and marginal positions which are not reducible to economic conditions (see Crespi, 1985, pp. 492 ff.).

4.5 STRUCTURAL POWER AND SOCIAL SYSTEM: THE CRISES OF POWER

Both outer and structural powers may be considered as two different aspects of the function of determination and adaptation of the social system, in so far as the latter is the result of symbolically mediated and normatively regulated social relations. As long as a social system succeeds in managing the contradictions, emerging within or coming from without, through successive adaptations and changes, we can say that the system is 'stable'. Being guaranteed by the flexibility that power can assure in dealing with the determinacy–indeterminacy relation, this stability may be understood by analogy with the concept of 'order through fluctuations' (see Prigogine and Stengers, 1979, p. 174).

Obviously, the degree of flexibility varies in relation to the conditions of the environment and the material resources available. From this standpoint the different social systems can be considered along a continuum, starting from the rigid 'closed' systems which characterize totalitarian societies, and ending with the flexible 'open' systems of democratic societies. However, one must not forget that there are in fact neither pure types of totally rigid and closed nor totally flexible and open systems. The *rigid* social systems actually function thanks only to the gap existing between the orthodox official forms and the practical relational dynamic (as, for example, seemed to happen in the USSR), while the *flexible* systems often function thanks only to the fact that their governments do not entirely comply, at the practical level, with the principles of pluralism and transparency which should characterize democratic societies (as, for example, seems to happen in the USA).

It is not possible to analyse here the different aspects of the relation between power and social system but, remaining in the perspective of the relation between the theory of power and that of social action, I shall comment briefly on the situations of crisis in which power can become involved.

On the basis of the presuppositions outlined above, the underlying causes of sudden change in social systems should be sought among the tensions and conflicts that any normative order, as a complexity-reduction form, will eventually fatally provoke. Another connected cause may be found in the failure of leaders to deal with the contradictions of the particular society they try to govern. Their inefficiency may be due either to the excessive absolutization of the dominant normative order that hinders the normal decisional and adaptive processes or to the excessive weakness of the same normative order that produces an unbearable degree of indeterminacy because of the arbitrariness of power, giving rise to the need of a more definite political regime. In fact, the two opposed alternatives may often be combined, as the tensions and conflicts threatening the prevailing order tend to diminish the balancing capacity of power, which seeks its own reinforcement both through increasing the absolutization of the forms of its own legitimation and through recourse to the pure indeterminacy of arbitrary decisions.

In the first case, the more that power relies on legitimacy, the more it loses its specific function of adaptation to contingency by decision. In the second case, the more that power appears independent of normative order and social representation and consensus, the more it loses its legitimation, revealing itself as pure coercion and violence. Both cases can be considered as aspects of the failure to manage the determinacy–indeterminacy relation which in the end will open the way to a new leadership.

However, if the objective weakening of the 'managerial' capacity of the constituted power is a necessary condition for revolutionary change it is not a sufficient one. Excessively rigid and coercive or too-weak powers do not always give rise to radical changes. If we consider the historical processes without too much ideological emphasis, we see that a real revolutionary event is quite rare. More frequently a leadership which appears to be inadequate to deal with the contingent social contradictions becomes integrated with new elements and is thus gradually transformed.

As the examples of the English, French and Russian revolutions show, the social system is never entirely replaced even in the case of genuine revolutions. Often the bureaucratic, military or technological ranks survive despite the change of political leaders and the innovation of constitutional forms (see Skocpol, 1979; Moore, 1966; Arendt, 1963).

These circumstances confirm that the power function can never be eliminated and that power is always grounded on effective capacities which are sometimes not easy to improvise.

4.6 THEORIES OF POWER AND THEORY OF ACTION

Although this is a sketchy exposition, I hope I have provided a good argument in support of the connection that exists between power and social action: the conceptual frame of reference developed through the phenomenological analysis of the character of social action in its relation to the symbolic-normative forms of mediation seems sufficiently articulated to guarantee the recognition of the ambivalence of power at both theoretical and empirical levels, thus avoiding the drawbacks of univocal interpretations.

Compared to other theoretical sociological approaches, the concept of power as the capacity to deal with the contradictions of the determinacy–indeterminacy relation and the distinction among inner, outer and structural power allows us to put together the different elements which these sociological theories analyse separately. Power can thus appear in the complexity of its opposed aspects of consensus and coercion, predictability and unpredictability, legality and illegality, reassurance and threat.

Compared to the functionalist model which stresses univocally the *consensual* character of power, as the general capacity to ensure compliance to normative obligations (Parsons, 1967), as 'concerted action' (Arendt, 1970), and as communication medium functional to complexity reduction (Luhmann, 1975), the phenomenological model adopted here shows that power has not only a function of control over the tendencies to indeterminacy that threaten the survival of the social system but that it can also be itself a cause of indeterminacy and disorder either *indirectly* (when it absolutizes the symbolic-normative forms, thereby losing its capacity of adaptation) or *directly* (when it makes unpredictable and arbitrary decisions).

Compared instead to the approaches which univocally emphasize the *coercive* character of power, the model proposed here shows that the function of power is necessary not only when there are conflictual interests but also when there is consensus about the collective goals. I refer here to those theories which consider power as an 'intentional production of effects' (Russell, 1938), or which define power on the basis of formulations such as 'It is said that A exerts power over B when A produces effects on B in a way which is contrary to B's interests' or 'A has power over B insofar as A can make B do something which otherwise B wouldn't do.' This well-known model includes various arguments by Lasswell and Kaplan (1950), Dahl (1957, 1971), Polsby (1963), Wright-Mills (1956) and Blau (1967). In this group one may also include the theories which rightly stress that power is often exercised not by decision-making but by *preventing* others from it (see Bachrach and Baratz, 1962, 1963; Lukes, 1974, 1978).

This kind of approach, which considers power as a capacity to make people do something or to prevent them doing it independently of their actual interests and wills, certainly has the advantage of stressing the imposition of power as a characteristic fatally connected with decision and coercion, but it does not give an adequate answer to the reasons why compliance with power is so widespread even when the interests of leaders and citizens are in opposition. This model underrates the 'negotiable' dimension of power relations, thus falling into the opposite misrepresentation with respect to the functionalist model. The common interest in the maintenance of predictable order and the tendency to avoid responsibility and risk often explain the readiness to comply, even against one's specific will.

Another aspect which the conflictual model of power tends to overlook is the fact that the function of power is necessary even when the interests of the leaders and citizens coincide: in fact, at the practical level there is always a problem of co-ordinating collective action through complexity reduction.

With respect to the elitist model of power (see Mosca, 1896; Pareto, 1966; Michels, 1966; Wright-Mills, 1956; Dye and Ziegler, 1975; Dye, 1976; Field and Higley, 1980), while there is agreement with the model that I have proposed as to the recognition that the power dimension can never be eliminated, there are many substantial differences as to the tendency to consider inequality as linked to the 'natural' characteristics of the leaders or the prerequisites of the social system. The elitist model does not sufficiently recognize the variety of the forms of power and the possibility of transforming power relations by a better allocation of power: the fact that power cannot be eliminated does not mean that it must always have the same distribution.

The phenomenological model of power is equidistant from the pessimism of elitist theories, which tend to justify dominance, and from the optimism of Marxist and anarchic theories, which, precisely because they are Utopistically orientated to eliminating power, end by favouring the totalitarian forms of power, as history has proved.

Finally, when compared to the structuralist model of power (see Althusser, 1965; Althusser and Balibar, 1968; Poulantzas, 1968, 1974; Foucault, 1977), the phenomenological model stresses the necessity to take into account the subjective as well as the objective dimension of power. As the analysis of social action shows, both the individual (as a product of society in his social identity as well as with a consciousness capable of distancing himself from objectivated forms) and the material and cultural conditions appear to be constitutive elements of the production of social reality, since they are at the same time *structuring* and *structured* dimensions in a circularity which can be interrupted only by the observer.

5
Problems of Method

'A final interpretation would be in itself contradictory. Interpretation is always in progress.'

H. G. Gadamer

The analysis of social action as a borderline concept of sociological theory leads to several methodological questions. I do not claim to exhaust them all by a systematic consideration. I shall merely try to point out some aspects directly connected with the hermeneutic dimension of empirical research.

5.1 HERMENEUTICS AND SCIENTIFIC DISCOURSE

Hermeneutics recognizes that the experience of truth is possible 'independently of the scientific method or even of those methods which try to follow science' (Vattimo, 1983, p. iv). As we have seen, life experience is the wider context within which scientific activity itself becomes possible and from which derive the choices orientating theories and research methods. For hermeneutics, then, there is no initial *tabula rasa*, no pure starting-point of thought, but the latter always begins within an historical tradition, a language, or pre-predicative and pre-judiced forms of some sort anticipating scientific discourse itself.

In this perspective truth, instead of mirroring reality, appears as an *event* or the 'original opening of a world' (Heidegger) which is historically and culturally qualified. What is known results from the encounter of different experiences within the *hermeneutic circle* where the temporal dimension is essentially relevant.

This approach stresses the reductive character of any form of knowledge with respect to the complexity of life experience, as *Erlebnis* which, being inexhaustible in itself, escapes any definite explanation. Life experience, as Dilthey, too, pointed out, is not commensurate with awareness but goes beyond what is clearly perceived by consciousness (see Gadamer, 1972).

The recognition of the relevance of the pre-predicative context characterizes hermeneutics as a dialectic of *translation* (and betrayal) within an historical *tradition* or as a *fusion of horizons* deriving from different cultures. This recognition is made possible by evidencing the impact of the symbolic forms of mediation on natural reality and on life experience itself. The same cultural impact is also at work in the selection of the problems and methods of scientific research: the way a researcher asks the relevant questions has priority for the constitution of any object of inquiry.

The analysis of the function of culture in social action, developed by the sociology of knowledge, has proved fatal to the idea of truth as neutral and objective: 'there are no facts but interpretations of facts' (Nietzsche).

The origin of hermeneutics, in the current meaning of this term, has been correctly placed by Gadamer towards the end of the last century, when the problem arose of the specific character of the historical and social sciences as compared to the natural sciences. However, as Gadamer has pointed out, Dilthey was still very much influenced by the model of natural sciences. But once the impact of historical tradition and culture on life experience had been recognized, any datum had to become a *datum of historical consciousness*:

> It is the unity of *Erlebnis* ... which represents the real unity of the datum. Within the gnosiology of the sciences of the spirit thus emerges a concept of life which reduces the pretences of the mechanistic model. (Gadamer, 1972, p. 92)

When the datum is understood in terms of a unity of meaning linked to life experience, knowledge of the datum appears to be a translation into objectivated forms of a meaning connected both to the original context of life and to its actual interpretation. Knowledge is thus an exchange among different interpretations, that is, an eminently hermeneutic activity emerging within the contingent conditions of experience.

After Dilthey the natural sciences would in turn be progressively influenced by the historical and hermeneutic approach. The dimension of meaning connected with life experience which is specific to the historical-social sciences shows that natural sciences research, too, is linked to everyday life and common sense; that is, to the intersubjective world of historically and socially shared meanings.

I cannot deal with the various developmental stages of the contemporary epistemology of science here, but it seems that today almost all theories of science, even those more distant from hermeneutics, are ready to recognize the relevance of the sociocultural context to the scientific discourse, giving credence to the conventional character of the presuppositions which are at the origin of scientific theories.

Particularly significant in this respect seems to be the development which started with the intent of Frege and Russell as well as the Vienna Circle, to ground science on pure logic presuppositions. Through the work of other scholars, such as Wittgenstein, Otto Neurath and Karl Popper, and, later, Kuhn, Lakatos and Feyerabend, for example, the epistemology of science ended by recognizing the sociohistorical dimensions underlying science to the point of considering the need of 'socializing epistemology' (Hesse, 1987).

The epistemology of Otto Neurath appears in some aspects to be similar to hermeneutics. According to Neurath, the methods of science are connected with language and tradition without ever reaching a final result or a total transparency: scientific discourse develops through various mutually influencing interpretations, and new theories give new significance to the previous ones. Stressing the impact of historical, sociological and ideological conditions on the development of science which in its complexity is never univocal, Neurath pointed out the 'unavoidable circularity of empirical knowledge as conditioned by its own methods of research and control', and the fact that the outer context 'influences the choice of the methods, the construction of theories and their historical success' (Zolo, 1986, pp. 38, 44).

I could easily quote many other similar examples, even referring to those authors who, like Popper, are more concerned to save the scientific specificity. The hermeneutic approach seems actually to be the horizon within which the entire scientific discourse develops, so that it is no longer possible to distinguish the sciences of the spirit from the natural sciences by referring to the historical and cultural basis of their presuppositions. The process starting from the scientific analysis of the forms of knowledge and culture has ended by recognizing that even that analysis was entirely made within culture itself, thus transforming our general conception of science.

In this same perspective the distinction between *explanation* and *understanding* on which, after Dilthey, the difference between sociohistorical and natural science was grounded, also seems to be obsolete (see Wright, 1971). As Ricoeur pointed out, we can now consider the relation between explanation and understanding no longer as antinomic but as complementary, that is, as moments of the same complex process called interpretation. If, strictly speaking, causal explanation represents the only scientific method, understanding appears to be the 'non-methodic' dimension which precedes, accompanies and follows any explanation (see Ricoeur, 1986, p. 142).

Showing the relations between interpretations of a written text, the theory of action and historical knowledge, Ricoeur points out that understanding gives a threefold specific contribution: to the deciphering of signs in the theory of the text; to the interpretation of the motivational intentions in the analysis of action; and to the capacity for following a narrative in the theory of history (see Ricoeur, 1986, p. 181). In this perspective, understanding appears to be related to our belonging to Being, a condition prior to any distinction between subject and object and to any objectivated form resulting from explanation. But, as we mentioned above, the dimension of belonging does not exclude the possibility of *distantiation* that develops through the objectivating method of science.

The fluctuation between belonging and distantiation, which we have already considered as specific to the pre-predicative character of action and the negative capacity of consciousness, is also manifest at the epistemological level in the relation between explanation and understanding, where understanding includes explanation while the latter is a partial analytic translation made by distantiation from the first.

Ricoeur correctly makes evident that the objectivistic scientific discourse, in its reductive character, implies several dimensions directly connected with that intuitive capacity which is at the basis of action. Life experience has a dimension which is beyond the reach of scientific objectifying knowledge: objective results can be obtained only by considering the situation of action from the *outside*, whereas understanding presupposes being *within* the situation itself (see Bellino, 1984, p. 138).

Thus the possibility of objectifying and analytically explaining reality appears to be a specific language game which, like any other language game, can only develop thanks to pre-predicative involvement into a form of life.

As I have tried to demonstrate in the previous pages, the sociological theory of action requires the maintenance of a particular tension between the explanation, specific to analytical sciences, and the understanding linked to the practical experience of everyday life. Both dimensions must be kept together, as one cannot be a substitute for the other. It is necessary to maintain this tension without removing it, either by absolutizing science as the only legitimate form of knowledge, or by dissolving any possibility of specific knowledge in a generic emphasis on common sense.

A mediation thus becomes possible between hermeneutics, which is not an 'anti-epistemology' but a consideration of the 'non-epistemological conditions of epistemology', and the objectivistic sciences. It appears, thus, against Habermas's critique, that Gadamer's rehabilitation of prejudice, far from giving up scientific rationality or leading to a mere subjection to tradition, allows us instead to use science within its boundaries and, precisely by recognizing that we unavoidably belong to tradition, to take a critical distance from it (see Ricoeur, 1987, p. 217).

In this same perspective we can also better understand the question of the relation between hermeneutics and the critique of ideology. As mentioned above, according to Habermas the critique of ideology can be grounded only on a rationality transcending the historical-social level and capable of denouncing the distortions of the latter. The concept of communicative rationality reveals the intent, similar to Marx's, to find a non-ideological point of view from which to judge ideology: the reference is to an ideal model of transparency free from any coercion and allowing the denunciation of any ideological fake.

Considering that it is not possible to give up the relation to tradition, hermeneutics believes instead that the distinction between true and false prejudices is possible only in the temporal distance which, in functioning as a 'distillation of meaning', not only eliminates partial prejudices but also enhances those which can help us to understand the concrete situation under consideration (see Gadamer, 1972, p. 348).

As Barry Barnes has pointed out in his analysis of Kuhn, the distinction between science and ideology has no firm foundations but becomes possible only through the differentiation between the context of scientific experimentation and that of political propaganda. When technical and productive activity prevails we speak of science, whereas when persuasive interaction is prevalent we are within ideology (see Barnes, 1982, p. 111).

Ideology tends to hide the limits of knowledge and to affirm truth, while science stresses its own limits and always considers its hypotheses as falsifiable. Popper's criterion of falsification, even if it cannot be considered in terms of reference to objective facts which are independent of interpretation, is still valid as a fundamental *attitude* characterizing science.

In the final analysis, any reference to an absolutely non-ideological dimension always implies the Utopia of freedom from any coercion, which reproduces the absolutizing certainty of ideology. The recognition of unavoidably belonging to tradition leads instead to the awareness that 'everything is ideological'. The only true definition of ideology in its negative sense must, then, be referred to the degree of absolutization of the cultural form: the more a cultural form is absolutized, the more it is ideological. In this context, if it is true that domination always uses ideology for its own purposes, it also appears that power generally has an ambivalent relation with ideology. Although the latter supplies legitimation for power, the function of power, for the reasons mentioned above, is in fact essentially based on a certain autonomy from the absolutized ideological forms (see Crespi, 1987, p. 89).

5.2 THE PHENOMENOLOGICAL ANALYSIS OF ACTION

In *La Sémantique de l'action* (1977), Ricoeur operates a distinction between the analysis of language which is orientated to *meaning*, that is, 'the whole of the objective forms within which experience is organized', and the phenomenology of action, which instead is orientated to *life experience*; thus any form of explanation of action, even the more reductive form which we find in the utilitarian model, implies reference to life experience as a dimension reducible neither to consciousness nor to the symbolic. If even the concept of purposive rationality implies a reference to the complex dimension of intentionality, Weber's concept of value-orientated rationality seems to imply a comprehensive reference to the horizon of life experience, which is always wider than the determined forms of interpretation of action by the actors themselves, their partners or the social scientists.

At the empirical level, the phenomenological analysis is an attempt to describe social action by taking into account the tension between the fact that action is irreducible to intentional meaning or to rules, and the need to determine social action in connection with predictability, identity and intersubjective communication. In this perspective phenomenological analysis develops as an attempt to understand the inner coherence of action, not merely by applying the rational or value-orientated models of the social observer, but also by trying to grasp the meanings of the actor's specific experience.

The opposition between rational and irrational is useless for this purpose, as it is impossible to identify beforehand one prevailing determinant dimension: the unconscious, the conscious will, the structure, actor's subjectivity, and so on. All these dimensions must be considered as components of the situation that has to be interpreted, since in the concrete experience the prevailing of one or another dimension is linked both to the actor's perception of the motivations of his action and to the observer's interpretation of the specific correlations he has established in order to understand/explain the same action.

Obviously, the interpretation of action cannot avoid either causal or motivational references, as well as the consideration of the material and structural conditions of the natural and social environment. But, coherently with the presuppositions aforementioned, the interpretation of action must also refer to the general elements and categories of action: reflexivity and the negative capacity of consciousness; the need for symbolic mediation; ontological insecurity; the search for identity; the ambivalence between identification and distantiation; the infinite character of desire and the non-coincidence between biological necessity and human need; the relations among Imaginary, symbolic and reality; involvement in the relation with things and others; the inner, outer and structural dimensions of power as functions of judgement, project and decision-making dealing with the contradictions of the social situation.

These general aspects do not fix any specific content or meaning of action, but at the same time they refer to problems which any social actor has to face in situations for which there are only provisional and uncertain solutions. These solutions cannot be predetermined but are potentially infinite, being the result of forms of action which are sometimes even opposed among themselves: as we have seen, the problem of identity, for example, can be 'solved' either by dependency on the dominant values of the social system or by autonomy from them, either by complying with the rules or by opposing them, and so on.

Within this context the purposive rationality stressed by the utilitarian or 'rational choice' models appears to be only one possible aspect of the complex experience which finds expression in social action, a particular dimension which can only arbitrarily be generalized for specific interpretative aims. The actor, although strictly linked to the social system which defines his needs and orientates his choices, should also be considered in his active capacity for transforming the socially codified values and patterns of behaviour, as well as the social structures and institutions, by distancing himself from the objectivated forms and *shifting* from one determined form to another. Thus sociality is not the result of a merely deterministic process but of a complex and contradictory life experience, never finding its entire expression in the codified forms of symbolic mediation on which social order is nevertheless grounded.

The historical forms of symbolic-normative mediation have been extremely varied, from the mythical to those of the culture of the Enlightenment or of technological society: no necessary relation can be established between the original exigencies and the determined cultural forms, even if in each of the latter the constant problems of the irreconcilable character of the social situation have found some temporary solution.

On the basis of these presuppositions it seems that empirical research has to develop through the hermeneutic analysis of the different components of action and by a constant exchange between social scientists and social actors: as a matter of fact, the connection between value orientation and empirical observation shows that the objectivity of the research, far from being grounded on the neutral mirroring of the thing itself, is based on the intersubjective communication between social scientists and between the latter and social actors.

It is along these lines that I shall try to consider some of the problems of social research.

5.3 SOCIAL RESEARCH IN A HERMENEUTIC PERSPECTIVE

Following Ricoeur's analysis of the text, social research in a hermeneutic perspective develops by taking into account, on the one hand, the concrete objectivated forms or 'traces' that action inscribes in history and, on the other hand, the fact that these traces, as aforementioned, lead to the manifold meanings of action as an 'event'.

Being at the same time both a concrete product and a sign related to something else, the trace has a twofold nature: as *objectivated form* it can be analysed in terms of cause–effect in its relation to a concrete sociocultural reality, while as a *sign* it has also to be analysed with reference to general categories of action.

The objectivated forms of action can be found not only in historical documents but also in the consolidated social structures (institutions, normative orders, patterns of behaviour and so on) as well as in the data of sociological surveys (questionnaires, recorded interviews and the rest). As I have stressed more than once in the preceding pages, action is not only the product of social structures and cultural models, it is also at the origin of these same structures and models. If the trace as an *effect* allows us to analyse action as the structured result of the different social determinations, the trace as a *sign* refers to the more complex processes where the creative and structuring dimensions of action emerge.

This is the reason why sociological knowledge develops not only through deductive and causal explanation but also through understanding interpretations, stressing the contradictions characteristic to the relation between the determinacy of social forms and the indeterminacy of action as such.

Starting from the twofold character of sociological research, I shall try to answer a number of general methodological questions:

(a) What is the relation between quantitative techniques and qualitative hermeneutic research?

On the basis of the presuppositions that I have tried to point out, it should by now be evident that hermeneutic research by no means rejects quantitative analysis of the objectivated traces of social action. However, the quantitative data should be considered within a wider frame of reference taking into account the manifold symbolic meanings of action and its ambivalent relation to the objectivated forms of mediation. Qualitative analysis is orientated to the comprehension of that wider frame through the interpretation of action in terms of its 'inner coherence'.

The limits of quantitative analysis are connected with the fact that survey techniques force us to make a certain compromise with our theoretical requirements. The tendency to consider as 'scientific' only what is measurable, prevents us from taking into account at this level many aspects that are essential to social dynamics. Quantitative analysis often appears as a *ritual* legitimating the scientific character of the interpretation and as a *fiction* linked to the necessity to determine the field of research by selecting only those elements which are susceptible of being translated into numbers.

The problem of the relation between quantitative and qualitative analysis should be posed in terms of the possibility of increasing the creativity of social research methods in order to make them more adequate to the requirements of the hermeneutic approach: as will become clearer in the next point, rather than use methods based once and for all on general and officially recognized criteria, it would be preferable to 'invent' methods for the particular aspects under study within the interpretative frame of reference.

(b) Traditional empirical research was mainly orientated to find *facts*, as objective aspects susceptible to falsifying the original hypotheses. How will this be possible in the hermeneutic approach, where there are no facts without interpretation?

I shall not develop here all the implications of this important question which has been discussed by so many epistemologists of our time, but I shall try to expound one aspect of it.

Some methodologists think that once the positivistic certainty of mirroring reality is lost, there is no longer any possibility of distinguishing scientific from commonsense discourse. If it is true that scientific method has nowadays become 'a tremendously vague thing' (Putnam, 1981, p. 199), it is also true that deepening the hermeneutic approach, which has always had so many links with Husserl's phenomenology, should teach us to go *towards things themselves*. The problem is not to think in terms of a datum independent of our interpretative activity, but to keep the tension between our interpretation and the 'otherness' which is offered to us when we put ourselves in a state of research. Starting from the recognition that prejudices are unavoidable, the hermeneutic approach stresses the importance of challenging our presuppositions by an active dialogue with what is foreign to us, with the unknown and unpredictable.

The *hermeneutic circle* – that is, the fact that interpretation is, at least in part, constitutive of the thing to be interpreted and is an exchange between different interpretations – is not, even in this case, a vicious circle entangling the interpreter and reinforcing his prejudices, but on the contrary, it is the attempt to establish an active exchange with the unknown without reducing it to what we already know.

To interpret means 'to let speak and to listen, without overwhelming the other' (Pareyson, 1985, p. 49); it means 'a humble disposition to find what we don't expect, more than what we are used to on the basis of our *a priori* models' (Marradi, 1982, p. 448). In short, it means to break our pure self-referentiality.

I am not overlooking here the many problems connected with the concept of 'otherness' if we don't want to think of it in terms of 'something waiting for us over there': the point is how to rationalize the interpreter's capacity to change, through listening and observing, his own analytical models which, as we have seen, are partly constitutive of the object to be interpreted.

In opposition to the positivistic approach, hermeneutics shows that there is no complete difference between the subject and the object, between the interpreter and the phenomenon interpreted: 'the interpreter has a founded pre-understanding, because he existentially belongs to a history co-determined by the same thing which he has to interpret'; interpretative activity 'lives in the space between what is familiar and what is foreign' (Vattimo, 1983, p. xviii).

As Ronald Laing has pointed out, any information is news about a difference. Sudden news of an overlarge difference tends either to be totally ignored or, if the news as such is accepted, we can't believe it, it seems unreal to us (see Laing, 1984, p. 361).

In the end the problem seems to be that of amplifying the interpretative capacity through the exchange of different experiences. In this context the knowledge of social processes has an analogy with the experience of the other: somebody who faces me claiming his own rights and forcing me to recognize him (see Gadamer, 1972, p. 14).

Provided that the tension towards otherness is maintained, there is no risk that hermeneutics will confuse science with rhetoric. On the contrary, hermeneutics develops a knowledge alien to any form of imposition: if the true empirical attitude is to be open to eventuality, then the hermeneutic approach appears to be a maximum opening.

(c) In the absence of absolute criteria of objectivity how shall the validity of social research be grounded?

Those who deny the scientific character of social sciences by arguing that these do not correspond to the scientific model of 'exact sciences' do not seem to be aware that the contemporary epistemological critique of science has deeply transformed the conception of science itself.

If, as mentioned above, the recognition of the fundamental historicity of knowledge specific to hermeneutics does not exclude the possibility of applying some of the current methods of experimental sciences to social phenomena, we must also recognize that in the new epistemological perspective even mathematics has been analysed in connection with the historical and social background (see Zellini, 1985; Di Paola, 1986; Hesse, 1987).

If we consider the various intentions orientating social sciences it is however true that their object, when compared to natural sciences, appears to be much more complex. While natural sciences are mainly orientated to the instrumental manipulation of physical forces, social sciences cannot leave out of consideration their critical and emancipatory aim. It would be easier, in fact, to establish sharp predictions of behaviour in a society conceived of as a concentration camp than in a free and democratic society where the variables at work are almost infinite. If natural sciences can proceed through drastic complexity reduction (even if nowadays we are more aware than in the past of the risks for our environment implied by that reduction), the social sciences have to take into account a greater number of dimensions connected with the quality of life. This is one reason why the social sciences cannot be primarily grounded on accurate measurements and certainty of prediction. A second reason is related to the dimension of meaning, that is, the fact that self-conscious actors, who are capable in their turn of interpreting their own situation, are the object of analysis.

The validity claims of the social sciences have to be mainly founded on the capacity to interpret social reality in order to establish an efficient relation with the social forces active in it. By 'efficient' I mean the capacity to promote social communication, to find out the unwanted consequences of the decision-making processes and the hidden tensions which are present in any social system, as well as to create the conditions for dealing better with the contradictions proper to sociality both by individuals and by social institutions. To what results considered as valid by the social community is our understanding/explanation of social phenomena leading us? To what extent do the interpretations of the social scientists, in meeting those given by the social actors themselves, produce stimulating effects of reciprocal adaptation and innovation? These are questions we have to answer if we want to establish the validity of sociological interpretation.

In psychoanalysis the communicative relationship between the analyst and the patient is not principally aimed at giving a correct definition of the patient's situation but at producing changes in the life of the patient through transfer. The validity of the therapy in this case is based, in the end, on the effects it has produced at different levels, and can only be judged by the partners in the relation, even if they cannot exhaust all of its meanings. Likewise, the validity of sociological interpretation should be based, in the final analysis, on its effective capacity to increase the power to rectify the distortions of social communication and to improve the management of the different social drives. The judgement about the efficiency of sociological knowledge can only be given through the practical evaluation of the social actors, social scientists included, taking part in the social processes under study.

(d) How shall we configure the social function of research in a hermeneutic perspective?

I have partly answered this question already, but for a moment I shall return to the relation between hermeneutics and the critique of ideologies.

In considering the linguistic dimension (*Sprachlichkeit*) as the essential medium of life experience, Gadamer stresses both the limits of language, as a definite code, and its limitless capacity for creating ever-new meanings. Thus the critique of ideology finds its ground in the recognition both of the finite character of the determined forms of expression and of the opening dimension of language as such: any cultural form hiding the reductive character of symbolic mediation is ideological to the extent that it is an attempt to remove that opening dimension through the absolutization of the current forms of expression. A removal which, in the final analysis, is always functional to repressive domination.

The essential function of social research is thus that of denouncing all the crystallized forms of symbolic mediation, showing the distance between the institutionalized social order and the real requirements of social action, and giving voice to the voiceless people who are not yet socially recognized. Through self-critique and the promotion of social communication, social research opens up social action to ever-new possibilities.

In this perspective social research has mainly the cognitive function of letting the unseen emerge, thus favouring the shift from one form of symbolic-normative order to another and forbidding any determined historical form to be taken as perfect or final.

Once the hermeneutic approach is correctly understood as stressing both the finite and the open character of language, the recognition of the unavoidable presence of prejudices appears to be the starting point of a comprehension which, through successive translations, transforms social reality by connecting the past to the present and the future.

As an essential hermeneutic exchange at the collective level, social research develops within society an active dialogue among all the different social actors in order to obtain a better understanding of the deep elements and contingent mechanisms underlying social processes. Thus social research reveals itself as pragmatically orientated to the renewal of culture and society in a perspective of emancipation.

6

Some Conclusions

The analysis of social action and power that I have tried to develop is not aimed at establishing a systematic theoretical framework but, rather, at clarifying some presuppositions for a better understanding of social action in its relation to structure and culture. Therefore, any conclusion formulated at this stage should be considered only as an introduction to further developments of the sociological theory of action.

I shall attempt just a summary of some of the results of my analysis which I consider more relevant for such a clarification, showing the possibilities they may open up for an empirical analysis of various social situations.

Starting from the recognition of the relevance in sociological theory of the distinction between human agency and social structure, there is certainly a convergence between contemporary sociologists towards overcoming the dichotomy of voluntarism and determinism. In this perspective many authors rightly try to interpret both action and structure as non-opposed but interdependent variables of a unique process. Without giving either element the dominant position, the different approaches consider action and structure 'as inextricably grounded in practical interaction' (Archer, 1990, p. 74).

Thus the debate on the relationship between human agency and social structure has developed in terms of differences in emphasis on particular elements and of the adequacy of each approach to represent and explain social dynamics. If we consider as an example the opposition between Giddens's 'structuration' and Archer's 'morphogenetic' approaches, it becomes apparent that the controversy is mainly about the degree of reification of the structures, their autonomy and their constraining character with respect to innovative action, the possibility of establishing when actors can be transformative and when, on the contrary, they are trapped into replication, and so on (see Archer, ibid., p. 78).

Although the current debate has greatly enhanced our theoretical awareness of the complexity of the aspects implied in the theory of action, I believe, as I previously said with reference to Bourdieu, Giddens and Alexander, that the recognition of the interplay between actors and structures is not sufficient to ground a theory of action. To say that action produces structures and is in turn conditioned by it does not explain the reasons for this interaction nor why action has an ambivalent attitude towards the structures. Only if we analyse the elements which are at the origin of that process shall we be able to adequately interpret the action–structure relationship and explain when action can be transformative or structure is excessively constraining.

In this perspective I have tried to examine three main points:

(a) the pre-predicative character of action which shows the incommensurability of action with respect to meaning (action as a 'borderline concept' of social theory);
(b) the necessity for determinate forms of symbolic mediation in order to ensure the social conditions of predictability and co-ordination of actions. The reductive character of the same determinate forms with respect to the complexity of action;
(c) the consequent ambivalence of action between the need for determinacy and the necessity for adapting the determinate forms of symbolic mediation (representations, norms, institutions) to the ever-changing requirements of life experience.

In this context I have had to deal with the problem of redefining the concept of subjectivity, taking into account the postmodern critique of the traditional subject. This has led to the definition of self-consciousness as a capacity to negate the objectivated forms, thus showing that the Self is constructed through the dialectic between identification with and differentiation from the objectivated forms. In this perspective the individual appears both as a product of society and as a potential active producer of new meanings and new practices by shifting from one to another form of determinacy.

On this basis the reference to some general categories of action in order to locate some recurrent elements of the relationship between actors and structures is made possible: the dimension of desire and imagination; the insecurity related to identity; involvement in the relation with things and the others; the transcendency of the existential horizon with respect to the social order. These categories can be used to locate the subjective aspects into which inquiry must be made in order to evaluate, with reference to the 'objective' conditions of contingent situations, the actual possibilities of innovation or replication.

But the most important aspect of the dynamic relation between action and structure appears to be ensured by the redefinition of the concept of power, consequent on the analysis of the contradictory situation of the actor. Thus power is considered not only, as for example in Giddens, as a generic capacity to 'act otherwise' or in terms of 'a dialectic of control', but also as a specific function operating within the actor–structure relation in its three different interrelated aspects: as an inner subjective capacity, as a social relation (outer power) and as a structural dimension.

As I said earlier, the conceptualization of the different elements relevant to the analysis of social action clarifies only the pre-suppositions of a sociological theory of action. Such a theory should translate into more definite paradigms those conceptual presuppositions in order to orientate the specific empirical analysis of contingent situations.

I have not elaborated on such paradigms here, but I would like to give very briefly an indication of how it would be possible to combine the aforementioned elements for an empirical analysis of social action.

The distinction between action and structure leads to the differentiation between the level of social action and that of social system. At the social action level, culture is considered in terms of the meanings actually influencing, through interiorized representations, values, rules, social actors (individuals, groups, movements, minorities and so on) in their attitude towards reality. At this level, on the basis of the recognition of the pre-predicative character of action, the dimension of desire and Imaginary, the degree of insecurity related to identity, the transcendence of the existential horizon with respect to the social one, as well as the evaluation of inner power as the capacity to deal with the contradictory drives to identification and distantiation, are particularly relevant. A low degree of inner power leads social actors to avoid the risks of unpredictability, and therefore manipulation by structural or outer power can be very high.

At the social system level, culture is considered in terms of objectivated forms of normative order, establishing collective goals, dominant values and institutional forms. The system structures are the result of the interrelation between cultural codes and the organizational, technical and economic resources as well as with prevailing forms of structural power.

The dynamic between social action and social system can be analysed in terms of the correspondence or non-correspondence between the different meanings effectively orientating social actors and the system's dominant values. Correspondence is not synonymous with consensus, but refers to the fact that the social actor's values do not differ from those of the social system to which he belongs. This does not exclude the possibility that the social actor objects to the practical functioning of the social system (as for example in the case of Savonarola's attitude towards the Catholic Church of his time). Correspondence, then, does not exclude all forms of dissent, just as non-correspondence does not exclude some forms of consensus, as may happen, for example, in opportunism.

Taking into account that consensus and dissent can be either active or passive (reactive), a typology of situations can be developed. For example, when the degree of correspondence is high, active consensus can find expression in forms either of extreme orthodoxy or of creative conformism, while passive consensus would take the form of routinized behaviour or adaptation. When the degree of correspondence is low, active consensus may find expression in different forms of opportunism, while passive consensus could give way to some sort of formal ritualism. Dissent, in a situation of high correspondence, will take the active form either of extreme traditionalism or of reformism, and the passive form of reactive deviance or eccentricity, while, when the correspondence is low, active dissent will give way to rebellion and conflict, and passive dissent to anomie or indifference.

To evaluate the actual possibility of transformative action it is also necessary to take into account the degree of rigidity or flexibility of the social system structures as well as the degree of their inner coherence. The ideal type of 'rigid' system can be defined in relation to the tendency to absolutize the forms of symbolic mediation and to the resistance to accepting change and conflict as normal features of social life, thus obstructing institutional issues of opposition. Transformative action in this case is more susceptible to assuming a disruptive and violent form: inner subjective power can develop mainly in opposition to the social system, while the weaknesses of structural or outer power will mainly be due to the incapacity to adapt to the ever-changing requirements of practical experience.

The ideal type of 'flexible' social system is by contrast characterized by the relativization of the forms of symbolic mediation and by cultural and political pluralism. It can give way to non-violent forms of conflict and is generally more open to innovation: inner subjective power can be promoted while the weaknesses of structural or outer power will mainly be due to the incapacity to provide social predictability and stable forms of identity. While sclerosis and alienation represent the ultimate risk for the 'rigid' system, 'flexible' systems are susceptible to ending in chaos and anomie.

Although rigid systems are perhaps more susceptible to coherence and flexible systems incoherence, coherence and incoherence are relatively independent of rigidity and flexibility, and the relations between these categories have to be interpreted time and again with reference to each concrete situation.

Along these lines, here summarized very schematically, the analysis of social action seems to avoid the drawbacks of univocal interpretation, giving new grounds for a critique of those theoretical positions which tend to absolutize either the deterministic dimension of functional order or the creative dimension of action. The reference to action as a 'borderline concept' allows us to analyse in their constant interaction both the subjective aspects of action and social system structures, showing social situations as a recurring problem of delicate balance between the contradictory drives to determinacy and to indeterminacy.

References

Aboulafia, M. 1986: *The Mediating Self*. New Haven, Conn.: Yale University Press.
Adorno, T. W. 1966: *Negative Dialektik*. Frankfurt a.M.: Suhrkamp Verlag.
Alexander, J. 1982: *Theoretical Logic in Sociology*, vol. 1. Berkeley: University of California Press.
Althusser, L. 1965: *Pour Marx*. Paris: F. Maspero.
Althusser, L. and Balibar, E. 1968: *Lire le Capital*. Paris: F. Maspero.
Apel, K. O. 1973: *Transformation der Philosophie*. Frankfurt a.M.: Suhrkamp.
Archer, M. S. 1988: *Culture and Agency*. Cambridge: Cambridge University Press.
Archer, M. S. 1990: Human agency and social structure: a critique of Giddens. In J. Clark, C. Modgil and S. Modgil (eds), *Anthony Giddens – Consensus and Controversy*. London: Falmer Press.
Arendt, H. 1958: *The Human Condition*. Chicago: Chicago University Press.
Arendt, H. 1963: *On Revolution*. New York: Viking Press.
Arendt, H. 1970: *On Violence*. London: Penguin.
Arendt, H. 1978: *The Life of Mind*. New York: Harcourt Brace.
Arnason, J. P. 1980: Marx und Habermas. In A. Honneth and U. Jaeggi (eds), *Arbeit Handlung, Normativität*, vol. 2. Frankfurt a.M.: Suhrkamp.
Austin, J. L. 1962: *How to Do Things with Words*. New York: Oxford University Press.
Bachrach, P. and Baratz, M. S. 1962: The two faces of power. *American Political Science Review*, 56.
Bachrach, P. and Baratz, M. S. 1963: Decisions and non-decisions: an analytical framework. *American Political Science Review*, 57.
Barnes, B. 1982: *T. S. Kuhn and Social Science*. New York: Columbia University Press.

Barrett, W. 1986: *Death of the Soul: From Descartes to the Computer*. New York: Anchor Press.
Bellino, F. 1984: *La praticità della ragione ermeneutica*. Bari: Ediz. del Levante.
Blau, P. M. 1967: *Exchange and Power in Social Life*. New York: John Wiley.
Bleicher, J. 1982: *Outline of a Positive Critique of Scientism and Sociology*. London: Routledge & Kegan Paul.
Boudon, R. 1977: *Effets pervers et ordre social*. Paris: PUF.
Boudon, R. 1984: *La Place du désordre*. Paris: PUF.
Boudon, R. 1987: Razionalità e teoria dell'azione. *Rassegna Italiana di Sociologia*, 2, 175–203.
Bourdieu, P. 1972: *Esquisse d'une théorie de la pratique*. Paris and Geneva: Droz.
Bourdieu, P. 1980: *Le Sens pratique*. Paris: Éditions de Minuit.
Bourdieu, P. and Passeron, J. C. 1970: *La Reproduction*. Paris: Éditions de Minuit.
Bouveresse, J. 1976: *Le Mythe de l'interiorité*. Paris: Éditions de Minuit.
Bubner, R. 1976: *Handlung, Sprache und Vernunft*. Frankfurt a.M.: Suhrkamp.
Calasso, R. 1983: *La rovina di Kasch*. Milan: Adelphi.
Carrithers, M., Collins, S. and Lukes, S. (eds) 1985: *The Category of the Person*. Cambridge: Cambridge University Press.
Castoriadis, C. 1975: *L'Institution imaginaire de la société*. Paris: Éditions du Seuil.
Cicourel, A. V. 1973: *Cognitive Sociology*. Glencoe, Ill.: The Free Press.
Crespi, F. 1976: Stratificazione sociale, classi e struttura del potere. In A. Ardigò (ed.), *Classi sociali e strati nel mutamento culturale*. Brescia: La Scuola.
Crespi, F. 1982: *Mediazione simbolica e società*. Milan: Angeli.
Crespi, F. 1985: *Le vie della sociologia*. Bologna: Il Mulino.
Crespi, F. 1986: Elogio della negazione. *Micromega*, 1, 186–91.
Crespi, F. 1987: Ideologia, potere e analisi del linguaggio. In F. Crespi (ed.), *Ideologia e produzione di senso nella società contemporanea*, Milan: Angeli.
Dahl, R. 1957: The concept of power. *Behavioral Science*, 2.
Dahl, R. 1971: Chi detiene il potere? In S. Passigli (ed.), *Potere ed èlites politiche*, Bologna: Il Mulino.
Da Re, A. 1982: *L'ermeneutica di Gadamer e la filosofia pratica*. Rimini: Maggioli.
Davidson, D. 1980: *Essays on Action and Events*. Oxford: Clarendon Press.
Derrida, J. 1987: *De l'esprit*. Paris: Éditions Galilée.
Dewey, J. 1938: *Logic: The Theory of Inquiry*. New York: Holt.
Di Paola, F. 1986: Gli impliciti culturali nell'adozione dei paradigmi matematici. *Rassegna Italiana di Sociologia*, 2, 287–300.
Donati, P. P. 1987: J. Habermas e l'equivoca forza dei mondi vitali 'razionalizzati'. *Rassegna Italiana di Sociologia*, 2, 299–307.

Dye, T. R. 1976: *Who's Running America?* Englewood Cliffs, N. J.: Prentice-Hall.
Dye, T. R. and Zeigler, L. H. 1975: *The Irony of Democracy.* Nord Scituate, Mass.: Duxbury Press.
Elster, J. 1985: *The Multiple Self.* Cambridge: Cambridge University Press.
Ferenczi, S. 1939: *Bausteine zur Psychoanalyse*, vol. III. Bern: H. Huber.
Ferrara, A. 1989: Verità, phronesis, autenticità. In G. Bechelloni, *Il mutamento culturale in Italia*, Naples: Liguori.
Field, G. L. and Higley, J. 1980: *Elitism.* London: Routledge & Kegan Paul.
Fink, E. 1966: *Studien zur Phänomenologie.* The Hague: M. Rijhoff.
Foucault, M. 1977: *Microfisica del potere.* Turin: Einaudi.
Freud, S. 1914: Zur Einführung des Narzissismus. In Freud, 1925, vol. VI.
Freud, S. 1917: Vorlesungen zur Einführung in die Psychoanalyse. In Freud, 1925, vol. VIII.
Freud, S. 1921: Massenpsychologie und Ichanalyse. In Freud, 1925, vol. IX.
Freud, S. 1922: Das Ich und das Es. In Freud, 1925, vol. IX.
Freud, S. 1925: *Gesammelte Schriften.* Vienna: Internationaler Psychoanalytischer Verlag.
Gadamer, H. G. 1971a: *Hegels Dialektik.* Tübingen: Mohr.
Gadamer, H. G. 1971b: *Hermeneutik und Ideologiekritik.* Frankfurt a.M.: Suhrkamp.
Gadamer, H. G. 1972: *Wahrheit und Methode.* Tübingen: Mohr.
Gadamer, H. G. 1976: *Vernunft im Zeitalter der Wissenschaft.* Tübingen: Suhrkamp.
Gallino, L. 1987: *L'attore sociale.* Turin: Einaudi.
Garfinkel, H. 1967: *Studies in Ethnomethodology.* Englewood Cliffs, N. J.: Prentice-Hall.
Gehlen, A. 1940: *Der Mensch. Seine Natur und seine Stellung in der Welt.* Wiesbaden: Akademische Verlagsgesellschaft.
Gerth, H. and Wright-Mills, C. 1953: *Character and Social Structure.* New York: Harcourt Brace.
Giddens, A. 1979: *Central Problems in Social Theory.* London: Macmillan.
Giddens, A. 1984: *The Constitution of Society.* Cambridge: Polity Press.
Goffman, E. 1959: *Presentation of Self in Everyday Life.* New York: Doubleday.
Goffman, E. 1961: *Encounters: Two Studies in the Sociology of Interaction.* Indianapolis: Bobbs Merrill.
Habermas, J. 1968: *Erkenntniss und Interesse.* Frankfurt a.M.: Suhrkamp.
Habermas, J. 1976: *Zur Rekonstruktion des historischen Materialismus.* Frankfurt a.M.: Suhrkamp.
Habermas, J. 1981: Dialektik der Rationalisierung. *Aestetik und Kommunikation*, 45–46.

Habermas, J. 1984: *The Theory of Communicative Action*, vol. I: *Reason and the Rationalization of Society*. Boston, Mass.: Beacon Press.
Habermas, J. 1985: *Der philosophische Diskurs der Moderne*. Frankfurt a.M.: Suhrkamp.
Habermas, J. 1987: *The Theory of Cummunicative Action*, vol. II: *The Critique of Functionalist Reason*. Cambridge: Polity Press.
Habermas, J. and Luhmann, N. 1971: *Theorie der Gesellschaft oder Sozialtechnologie*. Frankfurt a.M.: Suhrkamp.
Heidegger, M. 1927: *Sein und Zeit*. Halle: Niemeyer.
Heller, A. 1974: *La teoria dei bisogni in Marx*. Milan: Feltrinelli.
Hesse, M. 1987: Socializzare l'epistemologia. *Rassegna Italiana di Sociologia*, 3, 337–56.
Hjemslev, L. 1943: *Prolegomena to a Theory of Language*. Madison: University of Wisconsin Press.
Homans, G. 1961: *Social Behaviour*. New York: Harcourt, Brace.
Honneth, A. 1982: Von Adorno zu Habermas. In W. Bonss and A. Honneth (eds), *Sozialforschung als Kritik*. Frankfurt a.M.: Suhrkamp.
Hough, R. 1980: *Lord Mountbatten: Hero of Our Time*. London: Weidenfeld & Nicolson.
Husserl, E. 1959: *Die Krisis der europäischen Wissenschaften und die transzendentale Phänomenologie*. The Hague: M. Nijhoff.
Joas, H. 1985: *G. H. Mead: A Contemporary Re-examination of His Thought*. Cambrige, Mass.: MIT Press.
Kant, E. 1913: *Kleinere Schriften zur Geschichsphilosophie, Ethik und Politik*. Leipzig: Meiner.
Kernberg, O. 1980: *Internal World and External Reality*. Northvale, N. J.: Jason Aronson.
Klein, M. 1952: *Developments in Psycho-Analysis*. London: Hogarth Press.
Kohut, H. 1969: *Die Heilung des Selbst*. Frankfurt a.M.: Suhrkamp.
Lacan, J. 1966: *Écrits*. Paris: Éditions du Seuil.
Lacan, J. 1986: *L'Éthique de la psychanalyse*. Paris: Éditions du Seuil.
Laing, R. 1984: La ricerca scientifica per la realtà perduta. In M. Piattelli Palmarini (ed.), *Livelli di realtà*, Milan: Feltrinelli.
Lasswell, H. D. and Kaplan, A. 1950: *Power and Society*. New Haven, Conn.: Yale University Press.
Lévi-Strauss, C. 1955:*Tristes tropiques*. Paris: Plon.
Levinas, E. 1972: *Humanisme de l'autre homme*. Montpellier: Roy.
Lewis, D. J. 1979: A Social Behaviorist Interpretation of the Meadian 'I'. *American Journal of Sociology*, 2, 261–87.
Luhmann, N. 1971: *Politische Planung*. Opladen: Westdeutscher Verlag.
Luhmann, N. 1975: *Macht*. Stuttgart: F. Enke.

Lukes, S. 1974: *Power*. London: Macmillan.
Lukes, S. 1978: Power and authority. In T. Bottomore and R. Nisbet (eds), *A History of Sociological Analysis*. New York: Basic Books.
Manciulli, M., Potestà, L. and Ruggeri, F. 1986: *Il dilemma organizzativo*. Milan: Angeli.
Mann, M. 1986: *The Sources of Social Power*. Cambridge: Cambridge University Press.
Marcuse, H. 1955: *Eros and Civilization*. Boston, Mass.: Beacon Press.
Marradi, A. 1982: Boudon: un sociologo che ha sbagliato specializzazione. *Rassegna Italiana di Sociologia*, 3, 445–54.
Mead, G. 1934: *Mind, Self and Society*. Chicago: Chicago University Press.
Michels, R. 1966: *La società del partito politico*. Bologna: Il Mulino.
Moore, B. 1966: *The Social Origins of Dictatorship and Democracy*. Boston, Mass.: Beacon Press.
Moravia, S. 1982: *Filosofia e scienze umane nell'età dei lumi*. Florence: Sansoni.
Mosca, G. 1896: *Elementi di scienza politica*. Rome: Bocca.
Pareto, V. 1964: *Trattato di sociologia generale*. Milan: Comunità.
Pareyson, L. 1985: Filosofia ed esperienza religiosa. In *Annuario Filosofico*, vol. 1. Milan: Mursia.
Parsons, T. 1937: *The Structure of Social Action*. New York: McGraw Hill.
Parsons, T. 1957: The distribution of power in American society. *World Politics*, 10, 123–43.
Parsons, T. 1967: *Sociological Theory and Modern Society*. New York: Free Press.
Parsons, T. 1968: The position of identity in the general theory of action. In C. Gordon and K. Gergen (eds), *The Self in Social Interaction*. New York: John Wiley.
Piaget, J. 1979: La Psychogenèse des connaissances et sa signification épistémologique. In M. Piattelli Palmarini (ed.), *Théories du langage. Théories de l'apprentissage*. Paris: Éditions du Seuil.
Pizzorno, A. 1986: Sul confronto intertemporale delle utilità. *Stato e mercato*, 1, 16.
Poggi, G. and Ryan, C. 1967: Arnold Gehlen e la teoria volontaristica dell'azione. *Rassegna Italiana di Sociologia*, 3, 366–80.
Polsby, N. W. 1963: *Community Power and Political Theory*. New Haven, Conn.: Yale University Press.
Poulantzas, N. 1968: *Pouvoir politique et classes sociales de l'etat capitaliste*. Paris: F. Maspero.
Poulantzas, N. 1974: *Les Classes sociales dans le capitalisme d'aujourd'hui*. Paris: Éditions du Seuil.
Prigogine, I. and Stengers, I. 1979: *La Nouvelle Alliance*. Paris: Gallimard.
Putnam, H. 1981: *Reason, Truth and History*. Cambridge: Cambridge University Press.

Ricoeur, P. 1965: *De l'interprétation*. Paris: Éditions du Seuil.
Ricoeur, P. 1969: *Le Conflit des interprétations*. Paris: Éditions du Seuil.
Ricoeur, P. 1977: *La Sémantique de l'action*. Paris: CNRS.
Ricoeur, P. 1985: *Le Temps raconté*. Paris: Éditions du Seuil.
Ricoeur, P. 1986: *Du texte à l'action: Essais d'herméneutique*, vol. II. Paris: Éditions du Seuil.
Ricoeur, P. 1987: Logica ermeneutica. *Aut Aut*, 217–18, 48–61.
Ripanti, G. 1979: Editorial in K. O. Apel, *Ermeneutica e critica dell'ideologia*, Brescia: Queriniana.
Rorty, R. 1982: *Consequences of Pragmatism*. Brighton: Harvester Press.
Roustang, F. 1986: *Lacan de l'équivoque à l'impasse*. Paris: Éditions de Minuit.
Russell, B. 1938: *Power*. London: Allen & Unwin.
Sahlins, M. 1986: Scienza sociale e senso tragico dell'imperfettibilità umana. *Rassegna Italiana di Sociologia*, 4, 505–31.
Sartre J. P. 1943: *L'Être et le néant*. Paris: Gallimard.
Scheler, M. 1927: Die Stellung des Menschen im Kosmos. *Der Leuchter*, vol. VIII.
Schürman, R. 1982: *Le Principe d'anarchie: Heidegger et la question de l'agir*. Paris: Éditions du Seuil.
Schütz, A. 1932: *Der sinnhafte Aufbau der sozialen Welt*. Vienna: Springer.
Searle, J. R. 1969: *Speech Acts: An Essay in the Philosophy of Language*. London: Cambridge University Press.
Searle, J. R. 1983: *Intentionality*. Cambridge: Cambridge University Press.
Skocpol, T. 1979: *States and Social Revolution*. Cambridge: Cambridge University Press.
Sloterdijk, P. 1983: *Kritik der zynischen Vernunft*. Frankfurt a.M.: Suhrkamp.
Smart, J. J. C. and Williams, B. 1973: *Utilitarianism: For and Against*. Cambridge: Cambridge University Press.
Taylor, C. 1981: Understanding and explanation in the Geisteswissenschaften. In S. Holtzman and C. Leich (eds), *Wittgenstein: To Follow a Rule*, London: Routledge & Kegan Paul.
Taylor, C. 1985: *Human Agency and Language*. Cambridge: Cambridge University Press.
Touraine, A. 1965: *La Sociologie de l'action*. Paris: Éditions du Seuil.
Touraine, A. 1973: *Production de la société*. Paris: Éditions du Seuil.
Touraine, A. 1984: *Le Retour de l'acteur. Essai de sociologie*. Paris: Fayard.
Tugendhat, E. 1984: *Probleme der Etik*. Stuttgart: Reclam.
Valéry, P. 1957: Variété. In *Oeuvres*, Bibliothèque de la Pléyade. Paris: Gallimard.
Vattimo, G. 1981: *Al di là del soggetto*. Milan: Feltrinelli.
Vattimo, G. 1983: *Introduzione*. In Gadamer, 1983.
Volpi, F. 1980: La rinascita della filosofia della pratica in Germania. In C.

Pacchiani (ed.), *Filosofia pratica e scienza politica*. Lanciano: Francisci.
Weber, M. 1922: *Wirtschaft und Gesellschaft*. Tübingen: Mohr.
Wellmer, A. 1974: The linguistic turn of critical theory. In H. P. Birne (ed.), *Critical Theory, Philosophy and Social Theory: A Symposium*. Chelmsford, Essex: Stony Brook.
Winch, P. 1958: *The Idea of a Social Science*. London: Routledge & Kegan Paul.
Winch, P. 1964: Understanding a primitive society. *American Philosophical Quarterly*, 1.
Winnicott, D. W. 1965: *The Maturational Process and the Facilitating Environment*. New York: International Universities Press.
Wright, G. H. von 1971: *Explanation and Understanding*. New York: Cornell University Press.
Wright-Mills, C. 1956: *The Power Elites*. New York: Oxford University Press.
Zellini, P. 1985: *La ribellione del numero*. Milan: Adelphi.
Zolo, D. 1986: *Scienza e politica in Otto Neurath*. Milan: Feltrinelli.

Index

Aboulafia, M. 8
Adorno, T. W. 36, 37, 38, 41, 103
Agassi, J. 22
Alexander, J. 21–3, 134
Apel, K. O. 39, 68
Archer, M. 133, 134
Arendt, H. 9, 30, 61, 116
Aristotle 3, 60, 61, 62
Arnason, J. P. 38
Austin, J. L. 31

Bachrach, P. 117
Balibar, E. 118
Baratz, M. S. 117
Barnes, B. 123, 124
Barrett, W. 7
Bellino, F. 122
Bentham, J. 2
Berger, P. 35
Blau, P. M. 117
Boudon, R. 18–21, 23, 91
Bourdieu, P. 30–3, 134
Bouveresse, J. 101
Brentano, F. 62
Bubner, R. 30, 52

Calasso, R. 95, 106
Carrithers, M. 88
Castoriadis, C. 85
Chomsky, N. 56

Churchill, W. 89, 90
Cicourel, A. V. 35, 56, 57
Comte, A. 3

Da Re, A. 70
Dahl, R. 117
Davidson, D. 6
Derrida, J. 65
Descartes, R. 1, 65
Dewey, J. 75–6
Di Paola, F. 130
Dilthey, W. 3, 64, 65, 78, 120
Donati, P. P. 47
Durkheim, E. 11, 12, 13, 37
Dye, T. R. 117

Eckhart, M. 81
Elster, J. 88

Ferenczi, S. 103
Ferrara, A. 95
Feyerabend, P. K. 121
Field, G. L. 117
Fink, E. 63
Foucault, M. 30, 118
Frege, F. G. 121
Freud, S. 7, 22, 34, 72, 82, 83, 102, 103

Gadamer, H. G. 55, 57, 66–70, 120, 123, 130, 131

146 Index

Galilei, G. 1
Gallino, L. 22–5
Garfinkel, H. 35, 56
Gehlen, A. 5, 6, 8
Gerth, H. 100
Giddens, A. 33–5, 133, 134
Goethe, J. W. 93
Goffman, E. 35, 53, 59, 60, 102

Habermas, J. 13, 22, 35–47, 53, 68, 69, 73, 123
Hayek, von, F. A. 15
Hegel, G. W. F. 93
Heidegger, M. 7, 49, 63–70, 75, 83, 90, 91, 92
Heisenberg, W. 48
Heller, A. 17
Hennis, W. 61
Hesse, M. 121, 130
Higley, J. 117
Hjelmslev, L. 53
Homans, G. 18–20
Honneth, A. 38
Horkheimer, M. 37
Hough, R. 89
Hume, D. 2
Husserl, E. 24, 38, 48, 62–4, 92, 128

James, W. 75
Jarvie, I. C. 22
Joas, H. 78

Kant, I. 62, 93
Kepler, J. 1
Kernberg, O. 90
Kierkegaard, S. 93
Klein, M. 101
Kohlberg, K. 37
Kohut, H. 104

La Bruyère, J. 1
La Mettrie, J. O. 1
La Rochefoucault, de, F. 1
Lacan, J. 30, 41, 83–6
Laing, R. 129

Lakatos, I. 121
Lasswell, H. D. 117
Lévi-Strauss, C. 30, 31, 41, 52, 53
Lévinas, E. 52, 92
Lewis, D. J. 78
Lorenz, K. 5
Luckmann, T. 35, 42
Luhmann, N. 14, 47, 108, 109, 113, 116
Lukács, G. 36
Lukes, S. 117

Manciulli, M. 99
Mann, M. 105
Mannheim, K. 22
Marcuse, H. 17, 22
Marradi, A. 129
Marx, K. 7, 25, 34, 36, 61, 72, 91, 123
Mead, G. 8, 35, 37, 76–8, 87, 103
Michels, R. 117
Mises, von, R. 15
Montaigne, M. 1
Moore, B. 116
Moravia, S. 2
Mountbatten, L. 89

Neurath, O. 121
Newton, I. 1, 2
Nietzsche, F. 6, 7, 34, 72, 120

Pareto, V. 22, 117
Pareyson, L. 129
Parsons, T. 14, 21, 23, 25, 26, 35, 37, 100, 110, 116
Pascal, B. 1
Peirce, C. 75
Piaget, J. 101
Pizzorno, A. 89
Poggi, G. 5
Polsby, N. W. 117
Popper, K. 15, 121, 124
Poulantzas, N. 118
Prigogine, I. 114
Pritchard, E. 22

Putnam, H. 128

Ricoeur, P. 53, 62, 64, 65, 66, 67, 71–4, 103, 122, 123, 124, 127
Riedel, M. 61
Ripanti, G. 74
Ritter, J. 61
Roustang, F. 41
Russel, B. 117, 121
Ryan, C. 5

Sahlins, M. 16, 17
Sartre, J. P. 8, 32, 86, 87
Saussure, de, F. 30
Scheler, M. 8
Schürmann, R. 49, 82
Schütz, A. 21, 24, 35, 42, 87, 101
Searle, J. R. 6, 31
Shaftesbury, A. 1
Simon, H. A. 20
Skinner, B. F. 18
Skocpol, T. 116
Sloterdijk, P. 49
Smart, J. J. 10
Smith, A. 2

Stengers, I. 114

Talleyrand, C. M. 95, 106
Taylor, C. 57, 88, 89
Touraine, A. 25–30
Tugendhat, E. 87

Valéry, P. 40
Vattimo, G. 70, 119, 129
Vollrath, E. 61
Volpi, F. 62

Weber, M. 3, 15, 21, 22, 26, 36, 37, 38, 48, 49, 50, 53, 109, 112, 124
Williams, B. 10
Winch, P. 55, 57
Winnicott, D. W. 104
Wittgenstein, L. 54, 66, 67, 69, 121
Wright, von, G. H. 122
Wright Mills, C. 100, 117
Wundt, W. 76, 77

Zeigler, L. H. 117
Zellini, P. 130
Zolo, D. 121